Gertrude Hoyt Memorial

ANTHROPOLOGY AND POLITICAL ECONOMY

ANTHROPOLOGY AND POLITICAL ECONOMY

Theoretical and Asian Perspectives

John Clammer

St. Martin's Press   New York

90934

ISBN 0–312–04345–7

Library of Congress Cataloging in Publication Data
Clammer, John, 1947–
Anthropology and political economy.
Bibliography: p.
Includes index.
    1. Economic anthropology.   2. Communism and
anthropology.   3. Production (Economic theory)
4. Marxian economics.   I. Title.
GN448.C63   1985   306′.3   85–2116
ISBN 0–312–04345–7

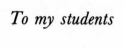

To my students

Contents

Acknowledgements

This book has 'grown' over a period of time, and it owes many debts to many people against whose ideas I have sharpened my own. Two of the chapters have appeared in print before: 'Concepts and Objects in Economic Anthropology', in my own *The New Economic Anthropology* (Macmillan and St. Martin's Press, 1978); and 'Economic Anthropology and the Sociology of Development', in I. Oxaal, T. Barnett and D. Booth (eds) *Beyond the Sociology of Development* (Routledge and Kegan Paul, 1975). Many of the others have been presented as seminar or conference papers in Singapore, England, India and Canada, but are published here for the first time. Grateful thanks to all those who requested them, stimulated them and put up with the evolution of my ideas, especially my students and colleagues in the Department of Sociology at the National University of Singapore.

JOHN CLAMMER

Introduction

Of the many movements that make up the contemporary anthropological scene, perhaps one of the most fruitful has been the 'rediscovery' of economic anthropology, largely as a result of dialogue with French neo-Marxism. The consequences of this movement have not, however, been confined to economic anthropology alone, but have extended, at least in some circles, to kinship analysis amongst the more traditional preoccupations of anthropology on the one hand, and of the opening up of new areas of inquiry on the other – including such topics as the the anthropological analysis of ideology, power, the state, colonialism and others. Somewhere between the two has come the revitalisation of topics that conventionally were felt to be somewhat peripheral to an anthropology proper – such as class analysis, social inequality and the continuing controversy over the so-called 'Asiatic Mode of Production'.

The essays in this volume are all in their various ways attempts to extend and deepen this movement, and to advance certain themes which I feel are important, probably even essential, to the continued viability of anthropology as a discipline and mode of inquiry. The first of these themes is the centrality of economics anthropology, a theme that derives from the belief that economic factors are basic in the analysis of social life. Inevitably such a view will appear to many as a confrontation with the popular idea that kinship is basic, at least in the so-called 'simpler' societies, and this question is addressed here. The second of these themes is that of the necessity of linking anthropology to development. It seems to me that far too much of anthropology is 'fiddling while Rome burns'. This is not an argument against the necessity for 'pure' research: rather it is the threefold claim that 'pure' research is best related to significant issues, that development is itself a major and absorbing field of investigation to which anthropologists can make a significant and probably unique contribution, that anthropology is a moral as well as a scientific discipline, and that consequently the anthropologist has no right to attempt to shirk engagement with the most pressing and critical questions of his era.

The third theme is that contemporary anthropology must engage itself in dialogue with Marxism. This is not, of course, to argue that anthropology must become Marxist, but rather that Marxism has thrown up a set of fundamental questions which even non-Marxist anthropologists cannot evade. Rather than stick our heads in the sand, these questions must be identified and responded to. The fourth and last major theme is that anthropology is not essentially but only accidentally concerned with the study of 'pre-capitalist societies'. This is just another way of confining anthropology to the study of the 'primitive'. In fact little of the contents of this book reflects this outmoded and limiting view, but prefers that anthropology is a mode of analysis applicable to the total range of human experience and its social expressions. Indeed, I would especially want to argue that the future of anthropology lies in its engaging the issues of the contemporary capitalist state and of everyday life in the industrialised and industrialising world. A corollary of this is my concern with the question of holism in anthropology, a concept to which much lip-service is (or used to be) paid, but very little is done in practice. What is presented here is in a sense new, but in another sense it is an attempt to return to a basic and traditional, but now almost lost, style of anthropology.

Certain theoretical and situational factors also inform the contents of this book. One of these is the belief that anthropology needs to be critical (or what has elsewhere been termed 'reflexive'), and as such needs to pay more attention than is generally the rule to developments in critical sociology, the sociology of development and the sociology of knowledge. Perhaps having always taught with, and alongside, sociologists is part of the basis of this, but it also springs from practical experience of the fruitfulness of such an approach. Another is the belief that too much anthropology is first-world-centric. Historically this is understandable, but things in the world have now changed somewhat. I have tried to present the elements of an approach that combines the traditions of the 'North' with the critical perspectives of the 'South'. Hopefully this also points forward to new themes – towards new models for the analysis of culture, of the anthropological investigation of alienation, of new ways of looking at the anthropology of 'complex' societies – and of others sketched out here. The 'project' of anthropology is always a pluralistically defined and evolving one. What is presented here is not intended to be the 'last word', but more an attempt to explore the fruitfulness of an approach integrated around the concept of political economy in the endeavour to demonstrate both theoretically and through case studies the viability of the anthropological enterprise conceived in critical terms.

Part I
Political Economy and the Anthropological Study of Development

1 The Concept of Political Economy: Political Economy and Anthropological Economics

A key factor of the study of development is obviously the economic. Indeed, there are those who would argue that *too* much emphasis is given to the economic at the expense of the cultural, social and ethical. Be that as it may, it does not diminish the necessity of elaborating a comprehensive anthropological approach to this critical economic sphere. As is commonly the case in anthropology, existing views on the relationship of development and anthropological economics are varied and eclectic. What I want to suggest here is that the current stage of theory in economic anthropology, and particularly the developments of the last decade or so, now allow us to formulate a fairly systematic, theoretically coherent and methodologically powerful view of this relationship: an approach which, in short, might be defined as *political economy*.

There are several important dimensions to this approach which I will try briefly to characterise. A traditional emphasis of anthropology, although not always one fulfilled in practice, has been that of *holism* – the view of the anthropologist's subject matter (human societies and social behaviour) as being something integrated, the facets of which (culture, kinship, political systems, systems of belief, economic arrangements), however much separated out for analytical purposes, actually form a single complex totality. More enlightened opinion currently holds that development too is a holistic phenomenon. Political economy, in recovering the anthropological notion of holism (albeit in a modified form), thus meets with development thinking at an important point of theoretical synthesis. Indeed, some economic anthropologists who have adopted the political economy approach would see their subject as inseparable from considerations of development, and, of course, of development seen in a holistic sense – as a process in which social, political, economic and cultural factors are inevitably and inextricably mixed.

Those who have followed recent debates in economic anthropology (for overviews see Dalton, 1971; Frankenburg, 1967; Clammer, 1975) will know that it has largely dominated by what has proved to be a mostly sterile debate between those who have become known as 'substantivists', who hold the view that economic principles are context specific, and their protagonists known as 'formalists' who declare, on the contrary, that economic principles are universal. This debate has never been satisfactorily resolved – mainly because it was formulated in terms that defied resolution. The political economy approach, however, has made it possible to transcend this particular internecine feud both by reformulating the problematic and redefining the basic focus of interest – not any longer the ethnographic analysis of individual 'primitive' economies, but rather of the radical impact of what is becoming or has become a virtually universal process – the penetration of capitalism. This has redefined interest in development along several new axes: the analysis of the unit of study not as a 'primitive economy' but as a *social formation*; the analysis of the corresponding concept of the *mode of production* rather than of 'economic processes', and of the coexistence and articulation of various models of production; renewed interest in social stratification and especially the question of how far the concept of class applies to the sorts of societies that many anthropologists seem to prefer; emphasis on the processes and social relations of production as well as those of exchange and distribution, and a concern with social dynamics and history – the impact of capitalism and its socio-economic consequences (introduction of money, redefinition of the concept of 'market', altered relations of production, etc.) being a historical and continuing process and one intimately tied in with other 'macroconcepts' such as that of colonialism. All this has at least two additional consequences – first, that it shifts emphasis in method from the older concern with microlevel, participant observation style fieldwork to include the methods of the historian, the economist and the sociologist, and secondly that it saves anthropology from the fate assigned to it by some of becoming the science of what is left over when the other social sciences have taken their pickings (e.g. Wolf, 1969). One symptom of this approach has been the rush to study the so-called 'informal sector' of developing economies in the belief presumably that the anthropologist is professionally stuck with being restricted to street-corner society, hawkers, slums and the other marginal zones of society.

It also implies interdisciplinary links, or, since in the context of political economy many conventional disciplinary boundaries are seen to be highly arbitrary, an assimilation of relevant perspectives from, in particular, the sociology of development. The sociology of development, and especially that whole school which has grown up around the various varieties of dependency theory, has had enormous impact and is itself a major impetus for the generation of a political economy approach. The intellectual history of this is too complex to go into here, but the essential point is that, whatever criticisms might be directed against it, the dependency approach has had a seminal impact and has been largely responsible for the immense broadening of the development studies debate which has occured since the 1960s. Within this broader context can be located the various forms of neo-Marxist thinking on development (including dependency theory itself) and especially the flowering of French Marxist anthropology, which, while not addressing itself directly to questions of development, has had great implications for the refinement of theory bearing on that field (Seddon, 1978 and Clammer, 1978). In particular, attention has been drawn to the problems of defining the key concepts of mode of production, social formation and articulation; to the historical dimensions of the penetration of capitalism; to the relative importance of mechanisms of production and of distribution; to the links between economics and kinship and to ideas such as class and rationality in the context of what used to be known as 'primitive' societies. Indirectly the debate also finds common ground with a revival of interest in peasant societies as a legitimate and indeed necessary subject of sociological inquiry and with a parallel interest amongst anthropologists in slavery (e.g. Watson, 1980 and Meillassoux, 1975).

What all this represents within the wider discipline of anthropology is a major departure from earlier conceptions of the relationships between economic anthropology and development. Amongst these would be the restriction of the anthropologist essentially to microlevel data and analysis, the idea that anthropology is some sort of handmaiden to the development economist and the concentration on the village as the appropriate level of development for the anthropologist to be involved in: in other words the old concept of 'community development' (cf. Dalton, 1971, p. 96). Related to this is the idea that by involving himself in such studies, the anthropologist can help to 'reduce the social costs of economic improvement' (ibid., p. 97). What essentially characterises this approach is a premise that is highly questionable in the light of the political economy approach: that the 'traditional' or conventional problematic of anthropology – that it is the science of tribal and village societies, bound to microlevel methods by participant observation – is in fact the correct or only one. What is additionally typical of this approach is its lack of systematic theory – rather 'middle range' theory is generated as the anthropologist goes along and as seemingly important problems present themselves within this paradigm –the impact of cash incomes, changing values as a result of modernisation, etc. Rarely are wider, contextual or *critical* questions raised.

The development studies question then has had an interesting impact on economic anthropology. It has shown up the inadequacies of the traditional anthropological problematic when it comes to dealing with such macroprocesses as development. It has shown up how dubious is the concept of 'development' itself, especially when it is reconceptualised as 'penetration of capitalism'. It has moved emphasis away from the virtually exclusive concern with microprocesses amongst tribal peoples. In short, it has remoulded economic anthropology and set if off in a new direction – but in a direction that is necessitating a thorough reconceptualisation of the premises and field of the subdiscipline. In turn this suggests that major methodological innovations will be necessary, and this is one area where economic anthropology needs to watch closely procedures being evolved elsewhere in the general field of development anthropology.

Certainly all this implies that economic anthropology is not simply a tool of development planners: it has an inherently critical dimension which should concern itself with the socio-cultural consequences of economic change, with indigenous definitions of development, values and the good life and with the theoretical critique and conceptual elaboration of development ideas, whether at the micro or macro levels. Nor is all this to suggest that a political economy approach to the contribution of anthropological economics to the study of development has no problems: it still has many, but discussion of the problems can only help to sharpen the focus. What is being said here is basically this: that the economic dimension of development is crucial, but *what* that dimension is and how it is conceptualised, related to issues of cultures and social structure, and how it is to be treated historically, needs to be explored in a holistic way. The traditional anthropological problematic contains, if often in an unapplied and half-articulated way, the idea of holism, but paradoxically because of the inherent limitations of that very problematic finds it very difficult to put ideas of totality into practice. This is in part due to its self-limiting to the tribal and microcosmic: the uneasy alliance that results in conventional attempts to relate anthropology and economics being symptomatic of this – there is no way really to do it without continuing to confine anthropology to an under-labourer role. Yet this is neither appealing nor necessary if economic anthropology is seen as a dimension of political economy. This has the additional advantage of dissolving many of the old distinctions between economic anthropology, applied anthropology and development anthropology while retaining what is valuable in all of them, and without sacrificing the critical perspective necessary in all approaches to the phenomenon of development.

REFERENCES

Clammer, John (1975) 'Economic Anthropology and the Sociology of Development', in I. Oxaal, D. Booth and T. Barnett (eds), *Beyond the Sociology of Development* (London: Routledge and Kegan Paul).
Clammer, John (ed.) (1978) *The New Economic Anthropology* (London: Macmillan).
Dalton, George (1971) *Economic Anthropology and Development* (New York and London: Basic Books).
Frankenberg, Ronald (1967) 'Economic Anthropology: One Anthropologist's View', in R. Firth (ed.) *Themes in Economic Anthropology* (London: Tavistock Publications).

Meillassoux, Claude (ed.) (1975) *L'Esclavage en Afrique précoloniale* (Paris: Maspero).

Seddon, David (ed.) (1978) *Relations of Production* (London: Frank Cass).

Watson, James, L. (ed.) (1980) *Asian and African Systems of Slavery* (Oxford: Basil Blackwell).

Wolf, Eric (1969) 'Kinship, Friendship and Patron–Client Relationships in Complex Societies', in M. Banton (ed.), *The Social Anthropology of Complex Societies* (London: Tavistock Publications).

2 Anthropological Theory and Development Studies: Some Critical Reflections

The purpose of this chapter is quite simple: to reflect on the relationships between anthropological theory and development studies, in particular as they relate to the ways in which development studies are taught in the Asian context. Anthropological theory is of key importance in this debate, as I shall argue, because of the increasing role that sociology in general is playing in the spectrum of subjects included under the broad rubric of 'development studies'. And if anthropology is involved in any form then theory is vitally involved, since the whole stance of the anthropological approach will be determined by the theoretical position taken and the ideological presuppositions that underlie it.

Since the term 'development studies' came into common usage as denoting a holistic approach to such problems as poverty, agrarian structures, industrialisation in its early stages and the relationships between the more and less technologically advanced nation-states, there has been a major move in two very significant directions: (i) away from seeing development issues purely or even mainly in economic terms, towards a political, moral and above all sociological approach; but yet (ii) the realisation that anthropologists who concern themselves with development issues need a grounding in economics and an awareness of the economic dimension of the political, moral and sociological problems. As I shall try to show, these two movements are not at all contradictory, but actually indicate a serious attempt to bring into being, especially in the context of the academic study of development issues, the much talked about but rarely achieved holistic

13

approach. Underlying this to a great extent is the quite correct awareness that a great deal of what passes for theory in economics is actually itself based upon assumptions about values, behaviour and relationships which are not made explicit, but which need to be if integrated thinking about development (and even about what is *meant* by development) is ever to emerge, and is to take on dynamic rather than static qualities.[1]

So far so good, but the question must immediately arise (assuming that we agree that anthropology has an important place in any development studies curriculum) of what *kind* to include and how it should be taught in a context far removed from that in which it was originally formulated. There is clearly a very real danger of perpetuating an intellectual form of that very 'dependency' which so much development sociology is concerned to criticise by teaching an inappropriate variety, or one based upon inappropriate theoretical foundations. So we must turn now to this central issue: the question of what kind of obviously precedes questions of curriculum content.

In doing this, I must first state what I take to be an absolutely basic axiom of all anthropology in the context of development studies: that it must be *critical*. In other words, the subject here cannot be identified either with a given body of facts (a simple empiricist approach), or with a given body of theory (which would make the subject simply ideological), or even with a set of techniques (methodology), since even the most seemingly objective techniques are actually subservient to a (usually implicit) set of theoretical assumptions. Rather the anthropology of development must be in a continual state of critical dialogue with itself (it must be a 'sociology of sociology') and with the world, and with the differences between its definitions of reality (which may well be western, class-biased, over intellectual, etc.) and those of its subjects (including the most humble peasant or artisan – or his wife or child). Anthropology itself, in other words, must be aware of its own location in the world and in the universe of thought, critical of its own concepts of man and society and aware of the links between its own theoretical activities and programmes of action by or for those it proposes to 'study'. (If this latter condition is unfulfilled its 'subjects' become 'objects' and one of the presumably primary purposes of the anthropology of development is thus radically undermined.)

The theory that underpins such anthropology will itself of
necessity be somewhat complex since it must include (i) a view of
the social, economic, political and physical world to which it is
supposed to apply; (ii) a 'philosophical anthropology' – a view of
Man and his nature and role in this world; a historical dimension;
(iii) a view of relationship between the theory and practice (no
sociology development theory can be a theory in or for itself
alone), and (iv) a mechanism for continual adjustment and
self-criticism. It must, therefore, be simultaneously both concrete
and critical – both of itself and the world that it is related to –
without being empiricist or trivial. This in itself, it should be
noted, does not *a priori* exclude all existing varieties of anthropological or sociological theory, whether the most formal (such as
structuralism, which is important for the understanding of the
macro features of society) or the most micro (such as ethnomethodology or phenomenological sociology, which may have the virtue
of explicating everyday ideologies which underly the grander
systems such as Marxism).[2]

A very real problem, however, still arises in relation to the
ideological assumptions or ethnocentric biases of many of the
leading schools of anthropological theory. These biases may be
intellectual – i.e. arising from culturally specific philosophical
positions – or may be situational, i.e. arising from the transfer of
theories from the well-endowed academic institutions of the
developed countries to circumstances and institutions in the poor
countries. Streeten, in a brief and thought-provoking article on
this subject, identifies five such difficulties or charges raised by
'developing countries against research on their problems and in
their territory by scholars from rich countries'. These five are: (i)
academic imperialism; (ii) irrelevance, inappropriateness, and
bias of concepts, models, and theories; (iii) research in the service
of exploitation; (iv) domination through a superior and self-rein-
forcing research infrastructure; and (v) (moral) illegitimacy.[3] As
Streeten goes on to point out, truth cannot be nationalised – it is
independent of the place or person who discovers or reveals it, and
it is the role of a critical social science to distinguish such truth
from the biases and distortions of any kind of intellectual
imperialism. In the developing of a curriculum in development
studies, two opposite and equally serious errors need to be
avoided: on the one hand, the uncritical adoption of non-approp-

riate foreign models and theoretical presuppositions; and, on the other hand, 'indigenisation' to the point of relativising or contextualising the perfectly valid ones (wherever they came from). As Streeten puts it, 'There may be an African economics, distinct from a European economics; there can be no African truth.' What is appropriate, however, is what has been termed 'participatory construction', or the systematic attempt to move towards a genuinely shared and integrated social theory (and not just shared empirical research or institution building).

We are moving now towards the classification of certain basic objectives, which can be summarised as follows:

1. The need for a large dose of anthropology in any development studies curriculum, which cannot be seen as essentially or exclusively an economists' preserve.

2. The need, however, to *integrate* anthropology into development economics and economics into development sociology. What is needed here is the fleshing out of Schumpeter's idea of an 'Economic Sociology' (a subdiscipline which to my knowledge exists in virtually no university curriculum known to me) or of the even older concept, which has recently begun to gain a new lease of life, of 'political economy'.

3. The need to define what elements of existing theory can be satisfactorally employed in the service of development studies.

4. The need to ensure that this anthropological theory, of whatever variety, is critical of the situations to which it addresses itself and is continuously critical of its own assumptions and biases of its own social location.

5. The need to define a concept of development. Again it is largely true that development seen from a purely economic perspective ignores completely the humanistic element in development studies. Presumably development is for people and the creation of the conditions of adequate shelter and nutrition, cultural dignity and self-fulfilment (however, *they* define these things). Lack of awareness of what would seem to be the obvious premise of the whole enterprise in past accounts for the shifts in emphasis within development thinking itself – for example, the recent return to emphasis on employment rather than growth, in the face of the fact that many programmes of economic growth have produced rather

than reduced unemployment and falling real incomes amongst the proletariat, and have worsened income distribution and promoted poverty and marginalisation.[4] That this concept of development must contain a sociological dimension would by now seem to be too obvious to need arguing about.

Certain concrete suggestions about the curriculum would seem logically to arise from this. The first would obviously be the incorporation of the five foregoing points in the syllabus itself. In other words, students, especially those who are experienced in practical development work, should never be expected to be passive recipients of some kind of received wisdom, but should rather be active participators in the definitions of the problems and the elucidation, and indeed creation, of theory. The second, which follows from the first, is that there will be major differences between the kind of development anthropology taught in the universities of the highly developed countries and that taught in the developing ones. A typical development course in the former case is likely to be devoted in large part to a survey of the currently fashionable theories about development (the various Marxist approaches, dependency, etc.), a certain amount of space will be devoted to analytical themes, such as the peasantry, the role of the military, and the remainder will be devoted to selected case studies, perhaps of Latin American lack of success in development and the Chinese experience as a model for other agrarian systems. Alternative variations will include material on industrialisation, urbanisation, possibly the role of education and educational institutions, and even perhaps some consideration of the now somewhat (hopefully!) discredited 'take off' theories and quasi-psychological assertions of Rostow, McClelland, Hagen and the like. In general, how the syllabus is constructed will depend not only on the regional interests of the teacher, but also very much on his or her ideological position. Such a course is usually directed at students who themselves come from the 'First World' and who have little or no direct knowledge or experience of the 'Third World', and quite possibly no intention of ever taking anything other than an academic interest in it. A well-organised course should, nevertheless, sensitise such students to the problems and provide them with a fairly adequate survey of exactly what those problems are and what and how people are thinking about them.

But to a student in a 'Third World' country, the situation is
rather different. He or she does not need sensitising – the
sensitivity is already and very significantly there. What such a
student needs is a course that is (i) relevant to his or her local and
specific social, cultural, economic, political and geographical
context; (ii) but which contains a comparative aspect, so that
other experiences and approaches can be considered; (iii) forces
the student to think theoretically and structurally and (iv) has
consequences and application for action. The essential problem
for the anthropologist here is perhaps in defining the relationships
between (iii) and (iv) – between theory and action. While a
knowledge of anthropological theory in general is necessary, it
should ideally be a *prerequisite* for entering the field of development
studies, which should really be a subject for the mature and
already well-educated individual from some other disciplinary
background. Any specific development studies curriculum needs
to be related to the other offerings available in the given
institution or country.

There are also implications here not only for the teaching (or as
I have suggested the 'creation' of theory), but also for the way in
which case studies are taught. Here two main points must be
made. First, the use of case studies at all can be dangerously
misleading unless the specific sociological and cultural conditions
under which they operate and the historical and political
conditions which brought them into being are carefully deline-
ated. We have seen in recent years innumerable attempts, for
example, to show that the 'Chinese model' is appropriate
elsewhere in the world, or that the apparently communal forms of
social organisation found in some societies can be turned into
engines for socio-economic development and political change.[5]
Such an approach must be used with great care, however, lest it in
turn becomes another form of 'imperialism' – the illegitimate
transfer of inapplicable models from one context to another. Such
models can be very seductive, especially as they prevent the
difficult necessity of hard thought in each local situation as to how
that situation really works and what it really needs. Such models
are, however, important for *comparative* purposes, but that is
another issue altogether.

Secondly, when case studies are used – whether as models or for
these comparative purposes – they should be analysed according
to the various criteria set out above and with a view to exploring

the reasons and constraints that determine how people behave as they do in those particular situations. A socio-cultural dimension is thus once again inevitably required, and as far as possible this dimension should be seen holistically. Discussions of poverty and employment, for instance, must be seen in not only a cultural but also in a political context. The results, when successful, are very enlightening.[6]

The anthropology of development then requires in some significant ways a renewing or reformulation of anthropology itself in several respects. The expansion of economic sophistication is one that we have already touched on. There are others: a concern by anthropologists with history; a heightened awareness of political science; a coming to terms with, even if not an acceptance of Marxism (many of today's seminal thinkers in the field are Marxists – for example, A. G. Frank whose *Sociology of Development and Underdevelopment of Sociology*[7] has been a major watershed in the discipline); and an awareness that ethics, both theoretical and practical, is part of the anthropology of development;[8] and a rigorous theoretical analysis of concepts – 'mode of production', 'articulation', 'exploitation', etc. Some have even suggested that this new marriage of sociology, history, economics and economic anthropology has actually taken us quite beyond the conventional limits of the traditional sociology of development altogether.[9] Certainly the failure of a good deal of sociological theorising to really come to grips with the very concrete problems of persistent poverty, rising unemployment, ethnic tensions, etc. suggests that modifications are seriously needed. The falling back on all sorts of vague 'cultural impediments to development' theories despite the complete lack of consensus and agreement about the basis of such positions would be another symptom of this general malaise,[10] along with the perennial resurrection of the 'Weber thesis' in one form or another without much progress being made towards the resolution of its problematic either.[11]

Part of the process of the renewal of development studies has come from outside itself – not only from events and institutional changes in the 'real world', but also from the evolution of the various subjects which go to make it up. One of these has been the rediscovery of the relevance of economic anthropology for not only exploring processes of development at the microlevel, but much more fundamentally for the clarification of basic concepts used in social, cultural and economic analysis – and for the reformulation of the idea of political economy.[12] In particular, the replacement of the old 'cultural obstacles to change' approach by a much more dynamic and structuralist one has been a quite significant achievement. Indeed, the challenge to anthropology itself posed by development studies has done a great deal to thrust traditional anthropology in the direction of renewal. The relationship between development studies (which is after all not a 'discipline' in any normal sense) and the subjects which comprise and surround it must thus remain as dynamic and dialectical ones.

This all suggests a set of priorities in the formulation of an appropriate development studies curriculum for use in Third World contexts. The first of these must be the production of a local and relevant case study and theoretical literature. The precise content of this will, of course, vary from country to country, and must be made available in the local languages. The production of literature by and from the First World about the Third World urgently needs replacement by production by the Third World for and about itself (and with which to educate the First World). This literature, however, must be at least as good as that coming from the well-funded development studies centres of the technologically advanced societies, and must, if it is sociological in nature, fulfil the conditions set out earlier in this paper. Secondly, an identification of the principal rather than the peripheral problems in the national and regional context must be made, since the total available range of problems, literature and approaches is very great. Thirdly, as development studies is a rapidly changing subject, provision needs to be made for the constant updating of the curriculum and of the knowledge and theoretical skills of the teaching staff (perhaps through regional seminars or a regional clearing house).

To date, most of these conditions have not been met. Courses in development studies (where they exist at all) are frequently a mixture of the currently fashionable theories (often relating to Latin America or Africa rather than to Asia), isolated case studies, and an assortment of analytical themes (e.g. urbanisation). In fact, no single course can contain all that is necessary to know – rather a series of linked courses would ideally be provided covering sociological theory, historical sociology, economic and political history, economic anthropology, political sociology and social psychology, as a prerequisite for the analysis of case studies and concrete situations, both through the literature and wherever possible through actual field experience, and leading always to an analysis of applications and courses of action. Naturally, this also implies an international perspective rather than just a national or even regional one, and it implies a willingness to set about a serious critique from the local perspective of the numerous and competing paradigms that abound in the sociology of development.[13] Indigenisation should never be taken as an excuse for parochialism. Likewise it must be expected that critical development sociology will meet with opposition. In the broadest sense of that term, it is a political activity, and to implement its findings takes political will and has numerous political implications and consequences.[14]

Certainly there are also approaches that should be avoided. One of these is the equating and confusing of development studies with courses on 'Social Change' and 'Modernisation' or 'Nation-building', which on examination turn out to be entirely different things. Similarly, courses on social policy or on urbanisation are often thought to be the same as, or substitutes for, specific courses in the sociology of development in the curricula of university departments. In fact, such courses are usually radically different in their content, intentions and presuppositions from courses in the sociology or anthropology of development, and rather than be confused with them should perhaps be considered preparation – since as we have asserted development studies requires a holistic and therefore mature and well-informed interdisciplinary approach. The 'modernisation and social change' approach is itself fraught with numerous theoretical difficulties – not the least being that modernisation can take place without development, that its equation with 'progress' is suspect, that its social effects are often negative, that it can take place in a context of political regression, and so on.[15] Such problems must be taken up, scrutinised and dealt with squarely by the kind of development sociology that I am advocating here.

Finally, it must be said that local Asian conditions can add a number of new dimensions to the 'classical' theories of development, in part because of their own unique historical conditions. Amongst these we might list the fundamental importance of cultural factors, the significance and dynamics of ethnicity and the major role of religious forces and institutions. None of these is by any means peripheral to development issues in Southeast Asia, and should be given serious study and consideration in any development studies curriculum. Equally, problems of qualitative development, social justice, traditional social, legal, kinship and land-tenure systems, the role of values and the exploration of alternatives (even perhaps seemingly 'utopian' ones) should be given a significant place in any balanced syllabus.[16]

In this paper I have been suggesting a number of (hopefully useful) ideas, in particular about the relationship between theory and development studies in general. I have, amongst other things, suggested the essential importance of an anthropological approach and component in development studies, but in the light of the equally important assertion that such an approach is only useful if it is of a particular kind (not always found in universities either in the developing or developed countries). Indeed, such an anthropology can only emerge out of a dialogue with the existing forms of development thinking – it is as much a question of evolving a new, contextualised, historically conscious, self-critical and action-oriented sociology (without it being, as we have suggested before, parochial or 'local' in the negative senses of the term) as it is of employing such a subject in the context of a relevant and concrete development studies curriculum. This activity is to a great extent a theoretical activity, since good theory is necessary to the production of sound knowledge and truth, and 'praxis' – the marriage of theory and practice cannot take place without a critical exploration of the foundation of anthropology, and a rethinking of the premises and applicability of many of its schools of thought in the light of the urgent needs of the developing world and its pressing problems. Most certainly anthropology in this context should not be seen as a set ot techniques (good for 'surveys', etc.), but as an equal partner in the development studies curriculum, and indeed as more than that – more as a *perspective* for the viewing of all developmental problems of whatever kind.

Certainly, this has not yet been done in many contexts. Theory is weak or non-existent; many universities have no courses at all in development studies; others confuse development studies with 'social change'. In many institutions the pressing issues of poverty, income distribution, unemployment, nutrition, healthcare, literacy, political development, personal and social autonomy, self-determination and participation, and cultural development, have scarcely been raised at all in the academic curriculum in which positivist and empiricist methods and non-Asian materials and theoretical positions prevail. How and why this is so would require another exercise in the field of the sociology of knowledge and the sociology of sociology and would necessitate a close scrutiny of the training of university faculties, sources of funding, the academic value system in general and types of officially encouraged research which cannot be persued here.[17] At the moment many of the research objectives are defined by the governments in the region not by the independent researchers, and social science research, rather than being critical (hopefully in a fully constructive way) becomes, increasingly, establishmentarian. While the link between national needs and development studies is necessary, a critical detachment is always necessary, since these very 'needs' are often exactly what requires discussion. The anthropology of development, when itself not irrelevant and underdeveloped, is precisely the discipline best poised to meet this situation.

NOTES AND REFERENCES

1. For an interesting example of a critical approach to this kind of problem see John Weeks, 'Fundamental Economic Concepts and their Application to Social Phenomena', in John Clammer (ed.), *The New Economic Anthropology* (London: Macmillan, 1978).
2. On this one point I must diverge from Peter Worsley, whose otherwise splendid paper, 'The State of Theory and the Status of Theory' (*Sociology*, vol. 8, no. 1, 1974), should be required reading in all sociological theory and sociology of development curricula. On this point of divergence see Beng-Huat Chua, 'Delineating a Marxist interest in Ethnomethodology', *The American Sociologist*, vol. 12, February 1977.
3. Paul P. Streeten, 'Social Science Research on Development: Some Problems in the Use and Transfer of an Intellectual Technology', in the *Journal of Economic Literature*, vol. 12, no. 4, 1974.
4. See for example Mahbub ul Haq, 'Employment in the 1970's: A New Perspective', *International Development Review*, December 1971.
5. For some critical views on this see my 'Anthropological Perspectives on Cooperation and Group Farming', in John Wong (ed.), *Group Farming in Asia* (Singapore: Singapore University Press, 1979).
6. See, for example, the excellent little case study by Benjamin White – 'Political Aspects of Poverty, Income Distribution and their Measurement: Some Examples from Rural Java', *Development and Change*, vol. 10, no. 1, 1979.
7. London: Pluto Press, 1971.

8. Essential reading here is Peter L. Berger, *Pyramids of Sacrifice: Political Ethics and Social Change* (Harmondsworth: Penguin Books, 1977). (First American edition Basic Books, 1974; English edition, Allen Lane, 1976.)

9. Ivar Oxaal, Tony Barnett and David Booth (eds), *Beyond The Sociology of Development* (London: Routledge and Kegan Paul, 1975). See especially p. 6 and the editor's introduction in general.

10. For a discussion of this area, see the paper, 'African Peasants and Resistance to Change: A Reconsideration of Sociology Approaches', by Caroline Hutton and Robin Cohen, in Oxaal, Barnett and Booth, ibid. pp. 105–30.

11. For some modest steps in this direction see my 'Islam and Capitalism in Southeast Asia', *Sociology Working Paper*, No. 63 (Singapore: University of Singapore, Department of Sociology, 1978).

12. See ibid.

13. A. Foster-Carter, 'From Rostow to Gunder Frank: Conflicting Paradigms in the Analysis of Underdevelopment', *World Development*, vol. 4, no. 3, 1976.

14. See Benjamin White, *Political Aspects of Poverty, Income Distribution and their Measurement* (1979), and Kevin P. Clements, 'From Right to Left in Development Theory: An Analysis of the Political Implications of Different Models of Development', *Occasional Paper*, No. 61 (Singapore: Institute of Southeast Asian Studies, 1980).

15. See Hans-Dieter Evers (ed.), *Modernization in Southeast Asia* (Kuala Lumpur: Oxford University Press, 1973), and especially Ever's introduction, 'Modernization and Development', pp. xii–xix.

16. For some hints about these themes see Nancy Chng (ed.), *Questioning Development in Southeast Asia* (Singapore: Select Books, 1977).

17. This exercise I have already attempted for Singapore in my survey, *Sociological Education in Singapore* (Singapore: RIHED, Occasional Paper, 1984).

3 Concepts and Objects in Economic Anthropology

In his Malinowski Memorial Lecture of 1971 Edwin Ardener claimed to have discovered or identified a break, a major discontinuity, between the concerns and methods of the prestructuralist anthropologies and those of the structuralist and post-structuralist ones which have succeeded it, of such a magnitude to justify the calling of the latter not a mere new trend, but an entire revision of the conceptual basis of the subject. As he says,

> I mean by 'new' that something has already happened to British social anthropology (and to international anthropology in related ways) such that for practical purposes text-books which looked useful, no longer are; monographs which used to appear exhaustive now seem selective; interpretations which once looked full of insight now seem mechanical and lifeless.[1]

Ardener traces the disjuncture between the 'old' and the 'new' anthropologies (I use the plural form deliberately) to the *connections* that the 'new' have with structuralism, regardless of whether the 'new' schools are necessarily structuralist in themselves or not. The conceptual gulf between the 'old' and the 'new' is held to be complete: 'The field of social anthropology is totally restructured.'[2]

For the economic anthropologist a number of important and provocative themes are thrown up by Ardener's paper, not the least being the question of whether economic anthropology (which is there passed over in silence) is to be included in the scheme of the 'new' order. Amongst other things, in the course of this chapter I will try to show that it is, and why it is. But the impetus to re-examine the basis and content of economic anthropology does not only come from such programmatic

25

statements as Ardener's, in which the ecomomic anthropologist is quietly ignored, but also from developments both within the subdiscipline itself and from external factors, including both developments in the 'real world' and in disciplines related to anthropology: in particular development sociology and political economy. Within the subdiscipline three features spring out at one immediately – the lowly position assigned to economic anthropology in the hierarchy of values of Anglo-Saxon anthropology (somewhere well below kinship, below the other 'special' anthropologies, but a bit above 'material culture') where it tends to occupy a sort of 'service' role; the sterility of a great deal of what passes for theoretical debate and has done so since the 'substantivists' and 'formalists' (of which more below) occupied the centre of the stage, locked in a battle which has either trampled more tender growths or has been so oblivious to them that they have bypassed the main arena and upstaged the old protagonists; and the sudden appearance from the outside of forces which have thrown the traditional procedures and problems into disorder, notably, first, the rise of a theoretically strong French economic anthropology and secondly, the related rediscovery of Marxism as a source of inspiration, and the realisation that the concerns of the development sociologist are far from irrelevant to the anthropologist in general and the economic anthropologist in particular. The resulting conceptual revolution is thus of significance for the subject of anthropology in general and, depending on your point of view, threatens to revitalise or engulf it.

But to understand and to justify the value of this revolution requires something more than simply asserting it; it also requires something of an explanation of its nature and of the conditions that brought it about. It furthermore requires a detailed investigation of its significance both in terms of its general theoretical implications and of its practical consequences. It seems sensible to consider the problems in this order.

Economic anthropology has had a chequered history, on the one hand, because of its slowness in differentiating itself from studies of material culture and primitive technology (and with a corresponding slowness in asserting itself theoretically), and, on the other, because of its highly ambivalent attitude to technical economics. While the history of social anthropology in general has solved the first problem for it, the latter is still a problem with which economic anthropology rather unsuccessfully struggles.

The pioneering compendium of Herskovits[3] did a great deal to establish the subdiscipline as a viable concern, the work of Raymond Firth in England did a great deal to consolidate it and the Anglo-Saxon debate since has come close to ruining it again. How and why? The answer lies at two closely related levels – in the selection of problems, and in the theorising of those problems, including their relationship to other disciplines (especially economics) and contiguous areas of interest. This is not, of course, to deny that the concrete achievements of the 'classical' approach have been considerable; the real issue lies in the clarification of the fundamental limitations of this approach given the basis upon which it is constructed.

The monograph containing the deliberations of the Association of Social Anthropologists on the subject of economic anthropology[4] reveals in a very clear and synthesised form the nature of those limitations. These may be summarised as follows: (i) a preoccupation, not with 'technical' economics itself, since none of these anthropologists appears to know any, but with the worrying questions of either *why* no anthropologists have bothered to learn any, or what the possible implications of such 'technical' economics *might* be for economic anthropology, if any anthropologists did know any; (ii) an overriding concern with the relationships of the two disciplines, but on the basis of an acceptance of the present problematics of the two. That is to say, that the question is posed in the form of 'what does economics have to say to anthropology?' or vice versa, rather than with asking the much more fruitful questions about the nature of the problems to be explicated, and the techniques and theories appropriate to this explication, regardless of the prearranged institutional boundaries. The significance of this should be more clearly realised when it is seen that the internal questions of the content and development of both subjects are currently controversial, and that what has been passed off as *theory* within a great deal of economic anthropology has in fact been little more than methodology mixed with a dash of self-criticism: no serious theorising of the concepts regularly employed has been attempted except in certain very localised areas. (iii) The failure to move in any systematic way from the recognition that economics in small-scale societies (as presumably it is in all) is deeply embedded in the other forms of social life[5], to an analysis of the actual articulation of such relationships of embeddedness. In practice, this particular corner of the field has been dominated by a variety of approaches ranging from that of Sahlins: 'A material transaction is usually a momentary episode in a continuous social relation. The social relation exerts governance: the flow of goods is constrained by, is part of, a status etiquette'[6], through the common view that the structural determinants of all 'primitive' societies are always kinship in the last analysis, to the even cruder view that 'sentiments' are the 'glue' that binds such societies together, as in the argument that the disadvantaged position of women in most cultures is a question of *attitudes* of a socio-cultural type prevailing in those cultures, rather than of socio-*economic* factors of a quite different category. On the other hand, however, it takes relatively little imagination to realise what fundamental differences of interpretation would emerge in relation to the classical ethnographies if (and if only for heuristic purposes) the traditional role of the kinship analysis was replaced by a comparable economic one. This is a point I will return to in more detail. A related concern has been the continuing attempts to *define* the sphere of the economic as *distinct from* other areas of social life. One of the results of this latter position, in its attempt to confine the range of application of the 'economic', has been the diminution of the value to be derived from using the term at all. (iv) An overriding preoccupation with the mechanisms of *distribution* than with those of production or with the larger structural features of the economy is perhaps the central feature of the 'classical' or 'liberal' position. This preoccupation needs to be divided into its component parts, since it contains several important elements. The first of these is the 'economics of the gift', that is, the problem, descended directly from Mauss, and Malinowski,[7] of the role of gift-like transactions, and particularly of reciprocal ones, in the economic and social life of a wide range of primitive and archaic peoples. The second is the view that

> One element in the analysis is common ground throughout –
> while the material dimension of the economy is regarded as a
> basic feature, the significance of the economy is seen to lie in the
> *transactions* of which it is composed and therefore in the quality
> of *relationships* which these transactions create, express, sustain
> and modify. Whether or not there is any agreement with
> Sahlins that in primitive conditions the place of 'transaction' in
> the total economy is more detached from production than it is

in modern industrial communities, the emphasis of interest is still upon the transaction rather than upon the production. Again, interest tends to be concentrated as much upon the set of ideas and emotional attitudes associated with the transaction as upon its formal qualities.[8]

The third aspect of this 'distributive' thesis is the central role that it gives to the market, both in the sense of the physical location in which exchange transactions take place, and in the sense of the *principle* of the market economy, i.e. the view of the economy as being the institutional area dominated by, or composed essentially of, exchange relationships. In practice this argument becomes extended (for example, by Firth[9]) to the claim that the economic universality of which the market principle is the expression does in fact exist, or (as, for instance, by Barth[10]) into the locating of the focus of institutional interest and of socio-economic change in the individual embodiment of the market principle – the entrepreneur.

Finally, some comment needs to be made about the extensive debate which has dominated wide areas of both British and American anthropology for more than the last decade – notably that between the so-called 'Formalists' and 'Substantivists'. The details of this dispute I do not want to enter into here – they have been very adequately summarised by Frankenberg elsewhere[11] but certain general comments need to be made, especially about the *nature* of this argument. The argument hinges essentially on the question of the applicability (or not) of economic theory to the economic processes of primitive societies, or, to put it slightly differently, of the suitability of primitive societies for investigation by the methods of formal economics. The apparent insolubility of this problem is a fairly clear indication that it is not the specific arguments advanced and counter-advanced that are in error, but the very premises upon which the whole dispute bases itself. It is even odder when one realises that, in the last analysis, both positions share the *same* premises, i.e. those enunciated above. In fact, the quality of insolubility which the Formalist/Substantivist dispute has stems largely from agreement about the essential validity of the 'distributivist' thesis and from a naïve belief in the necessary applicability and adequacy of formal economic theory and analysis when applied to those kinds of societies in which it has arisen and which it purports to explain. Also, in part, the problem arises from the wholly abstract nature of the way in which the difficulties in question are posed, namely, that questions about economic rationality or values, when discussed in terms of rationality or value theory *in general* become not only unmanageable, but also become philosophical rather than anthropological questions at the same time. A reading of Polanyi (the major source of the 'substantivists') indeed reinforces the feeling that the dispute is a philosophical one, but one not recognised as such.[12] Many of these points will be developed more fully below; the purpose of the present discussion is both to summarise the point to which Anglo-American 'classical' economic anthropology has brought us in theoretical terms, and thereby to know the base line from which the very radical new advances depart.

Even Sahlins, who in many respects provides the most vigorous attack[13] on the absurdity of applying in a universal way the 'theoretical outlook relevant to historically recent, evolutionarily advanced systems of production and exchange', fails to draw the obvious conclusions, but falls back on the argument that 'primitive economic behaviour is largely an aspect of kinship behaviour, and is therefore organized by means completely different from capitalist production and market transactions'.[14] Three difficulties reside in this position: (i) that the central role of kinship itself in the ideology of classical anthropology is accepted and reinforced; (ii) that a particular and debateable (in a very critical sense) view of the relationship between kinship and the economy is postulated in advance of any systematic investigation of the *actual* nature of these relationships; and (iii) that the exceptionally dangerous view is derived from this that if the theoretical apparatus of classical (i.e. capitalist) economics is *not* applicable in the anthropological field (something incidentially which cannot be determined *a priori*), then not only does capitalism not exist outside its historical and geographical heartlands, except where it is imposed as an alien system, but (and here lies the fallacy) *relations of production* identical with, or closely similar to, those characterising the capitalist mode of production also do not exist outside that particular and structurally peculiar mode of production. It is but a small step from this position to the claims that, first, class relations are a characteristic only of capitalism; where capitalism does not exist neither do class relations (even of a different kind), largely because of the subsidiary claim that in primitive societies differential access to wealth is *not* related to questions of rank, status and power. Secondly, that relations of exploitation do not occur within the productive situations discovered in such societies. And thirdly, that the primitive exchange economy, and particularly its quality of reciprocity, means that the capacity of the economy is limited, so surpluses of any great size do not appear. Sahlins himself thus sees socio-economic development in an evolutionary framework, and moreover one which is essentially technologically determined and ecologically based – high productivity which is predicated upon a suitable ecology and technological capacity is the *cause* of a differentiated economy and the increase of chiefly power.[15]

Frankenberg, in concluding his excellent summary of the recent history of Anglo-American economic anthropology, makes two important points: first, that the whole history of the subject up until the appearance of the 'new' anthropology is not a history of errors, but a legitimate attempt to grapple with the issues generated by a particular problematic. And secondly, and quite independently of all the French economic anthropologists except Godelier, he argues that, 'I suspect some economists would welcome the opportunity of rediscovering Marxist views on development without the embarrassment of getting them from Marx.'[16] Here he touches on a vital issue – that economic anthropology which is not the study of development is nothing; the alternative is the static approach – namely, that which is concerned with the properties of equilibrium states, is alien both to the situation of the facts that it studies in the real world, and, as I shall further argue, to the whole purpose of the activity if it is to be worth doing. As Frankenberg concludes:

> Such a model, I believe, could be constructed if one took as the starting point not the social concomitants of exchange but the social concomitants of production (including exchange as one of these).
>
> The key questions are: what is produced, by what social groups? How are the groups organized and by whom? What is the purpose of production (e.g. use or exchange)? How are conflicts which arise in the process of production dealt with? What alternative uses could be given to time used in production? If we ask these specifically sociological questions about technological change, two things will follow. First, we shall rediscover that the interrelations of technology and society are very complicated, which is no surprise. Secondly,

the exogenous comparative statics of cultural evolution can be transformed into a view of dynamic change, initially within individual societies and ultimately to a more sophisticated theory of social evolution.[17]

It is also worth remembering, in the light of this question, that the crediting of the new 'French School' of economic anthropologists with the distinction of having moved the focus of concentration from processes of distribution, is not strictly true. Frankenberg must, at the very least, be credited with the independent formulation of this particular idea.

The impetus that the French economic anthropologists have given to the reformulation and revival of the subdiscipline as a central force in anthropology as a whole, is huge, if as yet incomplete and rather undigested. The French group, however, certainly as it has so far appeared in the English-reading world, is far from comprising a united front. The broad divide is perhaps into those most influenced by Althusser, such as Meillassoux, Rey, Dupré and Terray, and those of a more eclectic and independent stance, such as Godelier. All have certain common roots in Marx, but the sense in which they do is one of the major areas of debate. While it is impossible to do ample justice to the full range of their positions in a brief summary, it is possible to determine certain key ideas which can be abstracted. In the case of the neo-Althussarians these can be represented as follows:

(i) A critique of 'liberal' anthropology concentrating mainly on that position's weakness for distributive systems, its belief in the universality and validity of classical or neo-classical economics and the projections of these theories on to its anthropological subject matter, such that, the characteristics of the economies of these societies are

> according to their postulate of the universality of capitalistic laws, necessarily, forms, if underdeveloped forms, of capitalism. Accordingly, the same concepts and theories used to analyse present capitalism are used to analyse any other economic formations. Any kind of assets (tools, land, manure, etc.) are 'capital' (Hill, 1970); any transfers of goods including stealing and giving, are 'exchanges' (Sahlins, 1965) if not 'trade'; any old man benefiting from collective work is

converted into an entrepreneur and calculator of marginal
returns (Firth, 1967); any kinds of returns are 'interests' whose
rate are sometimes computed as being 100% (Boas, 1897;
Mauss, 1950); such institutions as the potlatch are described in
terms of wild stock-market speculation (Boas, 1897), etc.[18]

(ii) Secondly, the claim that Marxism has a lot to teach economic
anthropology, but not the Marxism of the Marx who sought to
establish a theory of the pre-capitalist economic formations, but of
the mature Marx of *Capital*.

(iii) The belief in the co-existence, within the various economic or
social formations empirically observed by anthropologists, of
(normally) several modes of production, *one being dominant*.

(iv) The attempt to theorise adequately the concept 'mode of
production' itself in order to make it an analytically useful
concept.

(v) The elaboration of a substantive theory of productive
relationships in primitive societies, seen here as essentially
agricultural, sedentary and of lineage structure (i.e. what
Meillassoux calls 'sociétés traditionnelles d'auto-subsistance'), with particular reference to the ways in which the cycles
or systems of material production and biological reproduction are
indissolubly interconnected.

(vi) The extension of the preceding arguments into a more general
theory of either the succession of modes of production through
time, or of their symbiotic relationship at certain given historical
junctures (as with the various manifestations of the 'plural
economy', but always with the claim that one mode of production
is always dominant retained as the central part of the explanation).

(vii) The associated claim that anthropology is itself, or must
become, an historical science, because the structures it observes in
the present are not static, and because a great deal of its data, the
roots of its explanations and the inspiration for its choice of topics,
must always lie in history.

(viii) And finally the claim (which is also central to the 'colonial
encounter' debate)[19] that anthropology has always been an
intensely ideological subject, but also claiming, perhaps unlike
the colonial critique group, that progress can be made only by
purging anthropology of its ideological impurities. The influence
of Althusser and Balibar on all this is plain to see.[20]

What I see as being the main criticisms of this position I have developed elsewhere.[21] Some additional points, however, also need to be drawn out. In the earlier discussion, while accepting whole-heartedly the conceptual advances achieved by this movement, and the laying of a basis for a systematic relationship with development studies and political economy, criticism was directed principally at the central but curious theory of the domination by male elders of access to women, whereby they 'guarantee the control of the demographic reproduction of the lineages' by way of their monopoly of power over the élite goods which control marriages, and over the redistribution of slaves, between the lineages.[22] What is curious about this argument is its practical and theoretical inability to even begin to support the explanatory load placed upon it, notably the central significance in any account of economics of the reproduction of the conditions of production, and thereby, of course, of the reproduction of social relations as well. The Meillassoux/Dupré and Rey theory, as a basis for generalisation, is specific yet ethnographically unidentified, patriarchal, evolutionist, conceptually vague in certain important respects (and especially in relation to the concept of the 'mode of production') and is of dubious standing when its premises are clearly set out, notably:

1. that goods produced by the 'cadets' are entirely controlled by the elders;
2. that 'social knowledge' is exclusively in the hands of the elders, while 'technological knowledge' is not (even if such a distinction is valid);
3. that the elders conspire amongst themselves and between lineages to retain this exclusive knowledge;
4. that thereby they control demographic reproduction (there is confusion between various uses of the term 'reproduction' and about the relationships between demography and kinship: the elders control matrimonial exchanges);
5. that they thereby control the reproduction of the lineages;
6. that (contrary to Meillassoux's original formulation) the elders do possess powers of physical coercion whereby they can reduce a cadet to slavery;
7. that, unlike 'ancient societies', relationships between lineages are not based on warfare or conceptions of property or territoriality, but on the 'exchange' and 'conspiracy' functions

between elders ('conflict takes place in a field determined externally by exchange between the elders');

8. that the relationship between 'economy' and 'social structure' is a relatively simple one, mediated by the concept of 'control of reproduction of the technical conditions of production' (which in turn involves a 'power' or hierarchy model of social relations where the Dupré/Rey/Meillassoux argument is to hold); and finally

9. that the claim that 'demographic reproduction appears to be the essential condition for the reproduction of the conditions of production in lineage society' is something more than the tautology and truism that it appears to be.[23]

Rather than pursue the details of these arguments here, we might more fruitfully attempt to draw out of the debate some guide-lines as to how to build constructively upon these formulations in order to substantiate rather than merely assert the claim that economic anthropology occupies a central, conceptual role in anthropology and has something of quite major significance to say about the real world. This we will now endeavour to do.

The most casual acquaintance with so-called 'primitive' economies reveals at once not only a fairly high degree of complexity in productive, distributive and consumptive patterns, but also the major significance of the linkages between different patterns of productive forces within any given society, between the economy of the society in question and its neighbouring societies (whether the links are through war, trade, kinship, patron–client relationships, etc.), and between the indigenous economies in general and the wider system of which they are a part. It is the failure to give full consideration to this dimension which to a great extent lies at the basis of the theoretical weakness of many classical economic anthropological approaches to peasant societies (and, indeed, of classical Marxist approaches as well), since the representation of such societies as essentially embryonic or underdeveloped forms of capitalism obscures not only their true nature, but also the nature of their historical role. (Concentration upon *primitive* economies is symptomatic of the failure to deal with the processual and the wider structural features of the economies of societies embedded in the 'economics of the real world'.) What is also implied by this, of course, is the absolute methodological centrality of the historical approach to economic studies.

Secondly, there is the major question of how to set about providing an accurate representation of the socio-economic structures of the societies adopted for study by the anthropologist. This problem has several interconnected levels, notably the general question of choice, i.e. why choose 'primitive' societies at all?; the significance of the central role of kinship studies in classical anthropology and of its methodological priority; the question of the adequacy of structural-functionalism, transaction-alism, equilibriumism, and the 'rituals of rebellion' approaches to the characterisation of whole social formations, including the internal links between the economy and the other aspects of social structure, especially given their minimisation of conflict, disconti-nuity of contradictions within the societies they claim to represent. It is in the light of this that one must understand Dupré and Rey's central argument that one of the main faults of 'liberal' economics is its obscuring of the true nature of dependence and exploitation, both within 'kinship societies', and between societies in the situation where two or more modes of production stand in a hierarchical relationship to one another. Exploitation for Dupré and Rey, as for Althusser, is thus the product of, or is defined by, a *structural relationship*: 'We propose the following definition of the concept: exploitation exists when the use of the surplus product by a group (or an aggregate) which has not contributed the corresponding surplus of labour reproduces the conditions of a new extortion of surplus labour from the producers.'[24] We may wish to argue with the details of this definition, but if the principle of it is accepted then it follows that exploitative relationships may exist in *any* socio-economic formation (and not just capitalism), when the correct structural conditions occur. Furthermore, the notion of exploitation is closely related to the concept of the 'mode of production', and can be linked easily to the ideas of relationships of dependency *between* modes of production where several co-exist, and moreover can be seen as a central element in the process of the emergence of *classes* when such 'self-sustaining' economies are brought into relation-ships with market economies. In Meillassoux's account (espe-cially his 1972 paper) the classic case of such a relationship is to be found in the 'dual economy' theory, a theory which legitimises a situation in which the two spheres of the economy in fact relate to each other by way of, and in so doing perpetuate, exploitation, dependence and inequality.[25]

A number of points which arise from this account clearly need clarification and expansion. Amongst these points we might include the definition of exploitation, for example, is it a structural relationship? What are the distinctions between commodity extracting and labour power extracting exploitation? Do relations of *dependency* necessarily imply relations of *exploitation?* Are *inequality* and exploitation necessarily related? To this latter point, for instance, Gordelier argues that they are not; not that is to say that there is a *necessary* or structural relationship between the two:

> The idea of surplus is still obscured by the notion that many people still hold that there is a necessary causality between the existence of a surplus and that of the exploitation of man by man. This raises the general problem not of the mechanisms, but of the 'principles' of distribution, since the latter can be either equal or unequal among the members of a society. One and the same society may, moreover, follow different principles; depending on the objects which are to be distributed. The Siane ensure equal access for everyone to the use of land and to subsistence foodstuffs. Luxury goods, however, such as tobacco and salt, depend on the initiative of each individual. As for actual wealth–feathers, shells, pigs – the material basis for ceremonial acts and for access to women, these are controlled by the elders of the families and the important men (bosboi), whose prestige and power they symbolize. But this inequality does not signify at all that there is exploitation of some by others.[26]

A second group of points arises from the clarification of the concept of the 'mode of production', one of the most overused and uncritically employed concepts in the vocabulary of economic anthropology. In this respect Terray's harsh criticisms of Meillassoux are well justified, since the use of the concept oscillates between the pole of the weak usage – the simple enumeration of the general characteristics of an economy – through to the strong usage associated with Althusser and Balibar, where it is defined again in structural terms. What quite clearly does emerge is that a mode of production, if it is to be considered an analytically useful concept at all, must include both forces and relations of production, and must include mechanisms of distribution as well as of production in the strict sense.[27]

A third group of points relates to the more centrally or conventionally anthropological interests in all this. First among these is the status of kinship. As Terray succinctly puts it:

> To conclude, it is unwise to assume an automatic association between the predominance of kinship relations and that of agriculture: the data from the Guro have shown that the social framework for agricultural production could be provided by the various forms of Klala as well as by the lineage system. In none of these cases could an analysis of kinship reveal the fundamental structure of the whole society. In a more general way, the process of making kinship into a single theoretical entity seems to me no better than the invention of 'totemism' so justly condemned by Claude Lévi-Strauss: it brings together under one heading systems whose position and functions are not the same in every socioeconomic formation. Some of these systems organize social life as a whole, while others affect only some sectors, and these again differ widely: in some cases it may be production, in others consumption, or in still others, marriage contracts. To give kinship studies a strategically decisive value for the understanding of primitive societies, 'kinship' must be understood as more than a simple combination of terms and attitudes, and kinship systems must be considered in their functional aspect as much as in their formal aspect: at this point the unity of the entity 'kinship' can no longer be thought of as given and has to be proved.[28]

What follows from this in practice is the establishing of the actual relationships which exist between the spheres of kinship and the economy. Since these relationships will vary radically from society to society this is clearly not a question of prescription-in-advance, but of renewed ethnographic investigation. Or put in a different way, it is not, as Meillassoux tends to suggest, a question of the absolute priority of the economic base, but a question of the determination of actual links, given that the economic base, and the politico-juridical and ideological superstructures retain a great deal of autonomy of their own. Thus while there are cases where kinship relations and structures are to be seen as expressions of essentially economic relationships, it cannot be assumed *a priori* that this is the general or usual form of this connection in 'anthropological' societies.

Secondly, there is the question of class relationships: can these be said to exist in 'primitive' societies? Again we might turn to Terray:

> If it is correct that classes appear in a pure form only in socio-economic formations dominated by the capitalist mode of production, this appears to me to be because the economic base in this mode of production is not only determinant, as it is in other modes of production – it not only defines the part played by each phase in the production of concrete social formations, it is also dominant and itself plays the principal part in this production. Mercantile production becomes capitalist when labor itself becomes merchandise. At this point mercantile relations cease to govern only the circulation of products between units of production; they penetrate into these units. The ability of the capitalist to set up a production unit under his management is derived from the purchase of labor from the workers; it is by selling his labor to the capitalist that the worker can, on the one hand, gain access to the means of production and become a producer and, on the other hand, obtain the means of subsistence for himself and his family. This transaction between capitalists and workers conditions the very existence of the production unit, for it is the only means of bringing together the various factors which interact to form the labor process.[29]

Which he goes on to expand –

> It is now clear why classes only appear in a pure form in socio-economic formations dominated by the capitalist mode of production. A class is defined by the function of its members in social production. However, it is only when the economic phase dominates the mode of production that this function can become the immediate principle of production of concrete social groups; as long as the relations of production are not exclusively economic this function cannot by itself account for the identity of social groups, nor serve directly as the basis for differentiating them.[30]

If this view is the correct one, and there are good reasons again on definitional or structural grounds for saying that it is, several problems remain – how do we in concrete terms *account for* the emergence of classes at particular junctures in the history of certain societies, and in the case of those societies which, according to the definition, are not characterised by the possession of classes, do we in fact have adequate analytical techniques for dealing with their particular systems of stratification? We have already cast some doubt on the equation inequality = exploitation. Clearly this needs extending to a consideration of the operation of hierarchical structures (e.g. the Caste System)[31] in this respect. Also we need to return to a point raised above in relation to Sahlins, notably, that even if class relations as such are a characteristic only of capitalist, and preferably well-developed capitalist, systems, this does not mean that it is legitimate to ignore, or to define out of existence on semantic grounds, socio-economic relationships and structural positions which are related both to differential access to wealth and to status and power, such that the former is the principal mechanism in determining the latter.

We return here to another interesting point. In attacking Godelier for claiming that 'Exploitation begins when appropriation of the surplus is effected without counterpart',[32] Dupré and Rey reject this position on the grounds that this definition is not only universal and therefore vacuous, but that it implies that when the capitalist feeds back his profits into his enterprise, then he is exploiting *less*. But when they come to define class relationships they say, 'We shall speak of class conflict in any society where one particular group controls the circulation of a surplus product in such a way that the circulation of this surplus product ensures the reproduction of relations of dependence between the direct producers and this particular group.'[33] This has two consequences – it implies that class relationships exist in all but a tiny minority of very simple societies, and is not therefore a useful way of distinguishing societies, and it contains a particular evolutionary twist, for here we see the roots of the State, or Morgan rather than Marx. What in fact must be recognised is that while production relations are based upon the labour of the producers, itself regarded as a commodity and qualitatively different from where this is not the case, nevertheless the definition of the production relationship is only to be derived from an understanding of the location of that relationship within the total structure of socio-economic relationships which comprise the society. The *isolation* of one moment or aspect of the cycle, or

totality, contradicts the possibility of a processual analysis; this is
an error of both classical structural-functionalism and of some
varieties of structuralism and, paradoxically, of a great deal of
neo-Marxism: just as the viewing by Dupré and Rey of the
relationship between the elders and juniors at a *particular point* in
the cycle of exchanges leads them to argue that there is a
relationship of exploitation present ignores the role of the cycle *as
a whole*, so the structural-functionalists in a different context have
argued for the priority of structural categories, for example,
patrilineality or cross-cousin marriage, even in societies where
subsequent empirical investigation reveals that statistically these
defined states or categories are often empty, as when descent is
seen to be cognatic, or where it is demographically or for some
other reason impossible to fulfil or even approximate to a
preferred or desired pattern of marriage.

   In a more general way the real question that lies behind this
dispute is that of the nature and purpose of anthropological
knowledge. Central to this is the anthropologist's selection of his
subject matter, both in terms of the societies he studies, and of the
aspects of those societies chosen for the closest analysis. We also
see very clearly that any attempt arbitrarily to restrict anthropology to a particular kind of society, to a particular kind of
technique or to a particular residual problem thrown up or passed
over by the other social sciences, is contradicted both by practice
and by theoretical inquiry. But while it is an easy and relatively
superficial solution simply to point out that intellectual boundaries do not necessarily correspond to institutional or academic
ones, this still leaves unanswered problems about the historical
role of anthropology, and the continuation of, whether changed or
unchanged, that role into the future. So while for present purposes
questions of the Colonial context and so on can be left to one side,
the question of the theoretical adequacy of anthropology as a
means of grasping the reality of the non-western world remains
critical, and, as the debates surveyed above indicate, is of
undiminished importance in the case of economic anthropology
specifically.

   It thus materialises that anthropology, to be rigorous, must not
only be historical but must contain its self-criticism or its internal
dialogue with its own ideological postures, not as ancilliary to its
main objectives, but as its own central and distinctive problem;
indeed this is the precondition of the possibility of substantive

achievements. The pursuit of this topic at one level, however, leads us not directly back to economic anthropology, but to epistemology, and I do not wish to enter into this aspect in depth at this point.[34] In particular relation to economic anthropology, several cautionary notes need to be sounded. One of these must be to point out the cul-de-sac, in both theoretical and empirical terms, to which Godelier's approach to the subject leads.[35] The reasons for this are threefold. First, his concentration on *defining* the economic at considerable length, a debate which issues in the startling conclusion that, 'Provided we do not reduce the significance and function of a service to its economic aspect, or deduce that significance and function from this aspect, the economic can be defined, without risk of tautology, as the production, distribution and consumption of goods and services, a definition not only so broad as to be vacuous, but also one which borders on the absurd given the examples he mobilises to illustrate this, in which all that they appear to have in common is that, 'In each of these social relations, whether or not money plays a part, the economic aspect is that of the exchange of a service for goods and services.'[36] One should also note that the definition is couched entirely in terms of *exchange* relationships. Secondly, Godelier's concentration upon 'rationality', as his central analytical category, has the consequence of committing him not only (and unconsciously) to a new variety of 'economic man' – the calculating, rational and logical pursuer of economic ends by rational means – but also to a corresponding relativity, since neither the ends nor the means are defined, all that is of interest is the consistency and logicality of the pursuit. Furthermore, this rationality may not even be conscious.

By way of all these analyses and distinctions some theoretical conclusions can be gathered together. There is no rationality 'in itself', nor any absolute rationality. What is rational today may be irrational tomorrow, what is rational in one society may be irrational in another. Finally, there is no exclusive economic rationality. These negative conclusions challenge the preconceptions of 'ordinary' consciousness and are remedies against the 'temptations' that these present. In the end, the idea of rationality obliges us to analyse the basis of the structures of social life, their raison d'etre and their evolution. These raisons d'etre and this evolution are not merely the achievement of men's conscious activity but are the unintentional results of their social activity. While there is some rationality in the social development of mankind, the subject of this rationality is not the isolated and absurd individual of a timeless human nature and psychology, but men in all the aspects, conscious and unconscious, of their social relations.[37]

Thirdly, while Godelier's text does attempt to bring into a systematic relationship anthropology and Marxism, it does so on the basis of an idiosyncratic view of the nature of both these two elements in his equation. As Asad rightly points out, 'Godelier accepts and reaffirms the theoretical practice of a particular part of anthropology',[38] but he does not go on to draw a conclusion from this, notably that in so doing, at a deep level Godelier renders himself indistinguishable from those he wishes to criticise – not only the substantivists whom he closely resembles, but even, paradoxically, the formalists, since logically the direction of his rationality argument can as easily point to a formalist conclusion as away from one.

But perhaps above all, and this is a somewhat different sort of point, Godelier fails to establish that his introductory claim has been fulfilled or even approached, notably that

In this search for the epistemological conditions of a rigorous proof, one conclusion became obvious at any early stage, namely, that the question of the 'rationality' of a system means primarily the question of the 'historical necessity' for its existence – in other words, in order to think out this question one has to construct the theory of the conditions for the system's appearance and development, something that is usually excluded from, or kept outside, the field of research of political economy and left to the 'historians' of economic life.[39]

This is very commendable, but in the context of Godelier's thought it turns not just upon his own fulfilling of his own project, but on the wider question of the status of history in Marxism, the status of Marxism as a theory of history, and of the location of anthropology within these histories. Godelier's insistence, not on a model of unilinear evolution, but on different structures (each of which however apparently irrational is in fact rational) evolving differentially or unevenly, raises a host of problems not just about the historicity of the 'anthropological societies' but of the whole theory of history which informs and ultimately governs the more obviously anthropological debate. For as Engels once said, 'The materialist conception of history also has a lot of friends nowadays for whom it serves as an excuse for not studying history.' It might also be noted that the idea of 'uneven development' is itself obscure and tells one nothing about either the dynamics or causes of the unevenness, nor about the direction of development of either the parts or the whole of the total system.

If there is a 'new' economic anthropology it is thus one which, while it has a number of common themes, does not as yet represent either a 'school' or a solution to what some people insist on seeing as 'the present crisis' in anthropology. It does, however, like Wittgenstein's philosophy which also actually only said very little, point in certain directions. And what these directions are appear not just from its positive claims but also from the lacunae which still transparently exist. These themes can undoubtedly be summarised.

First, and methodologically, economic anthropology has been, and is being, drawn closer to structuralism as a result of the influence of Althusser rather than Lévi-Strauss, the expectations that structuralism's own totalising technique is applicable in this field, and also because of the epistemological links. The new economic anthropology, like structuralism, is to a great extent concerned with the rigorous theorising of its operational concepts as well as with moving the whole level of analysis from the phenomenal to a more fundamental explanatory level. Or put in a different way, in the new economic anthropology, the question of what is 'empirical' is as problematic as it is in structuralism, or for that matter, in Marxism. Other aspects of this are the requirements of 'holism', the requirement that history be regarded not as an additional luxury in which the anthropologist may or may not indulge at will, but a central requirement for adequate explanation, the requirement that the old disciplinary boundaries, especially between anthropology and economics and sociology be largely ignored, and the requirement that economic anthropology ally itself firmly with development studies, since this is clearly where both its problems and its most pressing conceptual issues lie. Since it can fairly be claimed that the main area of debate within substantive economic anthropology resides in the problem of *value*, the ideas that the anthropologist can pass to the sociologist or economist of development are also central, and in particular the question 'What *is* development?'

NOTES AND REFERENCES

1. E. Ardener, 'The New Anthropology and Its Critics', *Man*, 6, 3. 1971, p. 449.
2. Ibid., p. 450.
3. M. J. Herskovits, *Economic Anthropology* (New York, 1952).
4. R. Firth (ed.), *Themes in Economic Anthropology*, A.S.A. Monograph No. 6 (London: Tavistock Publications, 1967).
5. E.g., ibid., p. 1.
6. M. Sahlins, 'On the Sociology of Primitive Exchange', in M. Banton (ed.), *The Relevance of Models for Social Anthropology*, A.S.A. Monograph No. 1 (London, 1965) p. 139.
7. M. Mauss, 'Essai sur le don', *L'Année sociologique*, 1, 1923–24; B. Malinowski, *Argonauts of the Western Pacific* (London, 1922).
8. R. Firth (ed.), *Themes in Economic Anthropology*, pp. 4–5.
9. Ibid. p. 6.
10. F. Barth (ed.), *The Role of the Entrepreneur in Social Change in Northern Norway* (Bergen and Oslo, 1963).
11. R. Frankenberg, 'Economic Anthropology: One Anthropologist's View', in R. Firth (ed.), *Themes in Economic Anthropology*, pp. 47–89.
12. K. Polanyi, *The Origin of Our Time: The Great Transformation* (London, 1946); and K. Polanyi, C. W. Arensberg and H. W. Pearson, *Trade and Market in the Early Empires* (Glencoe, Ill., 1957).
13. M. Sahlins, 'Political Power and the Economy in Primitive Society', in G. E. Dole and R. L. Carneiro, *Essays in the Science of Culture* (N.Y., 1960) pp. 390–415.
14. Ibid., p. 391.
15. Ibid. and his *Social Stratification in Polynesia* (Seattle, Washington, 1958).
16. Frankenberg, 'Economic Anthropology: One Anthropologist's View', p. 84.
17. Ibid., p. 84.
18. C. Meillassoux, 'From Reproduction to Production', *Economy and Society*, vol. 1, no. 1, 1972, p. 93. See also G. Dupré and P. P. Rey, 'Reflections on the Pertinence of a Theory of the History of Exchange', *Economy and Society*, vol. 2, no. 2, 1973; E. Terray, *Marxism and 'Primitive' Societies* (London and New York, 1972); C. Meillassoux, 'Essai d'interpretation du phénomène économique dans les sociétés traditionnelles d'autosubsistance', *Cahiers d'Études Africaines*, 1960.
19. See T. Asad (ed.) *Anthropology and the Colonial Encounter* (London, 1973).
20. See especially L. Althusser and E. Balibar, *Reading Capital* (London, 1970).
21. J. R. Clammer, 'Economic Anthropology and the Sociology of Development: "Liberal" Anthropology and its French critics', in I. Oxaal, T. Barnett, D. Booth (eds), *Beyond the Sociology of Development* (London, 1975).
22. Ibid., pp. 215 ff.
23. Ibid., pp. 219–220.

46 *Political Economy and the Study of Development*

24. Dupré and Rey, 'Reflections on the Pertinence of a Theory of the History of Exchange', p. 152.
25. Meillassoux, 'From Reproduction to Production', and his 'Imperialism as a Mode of Reproduction of Labour Power', 1974.
26. M. Godelier, *Rationality and Irrationality in Economics* (London, 1972), p. 275.
27. See Terray, *Marxism and 'Primitive' Societies*, pp. 97–8 and Clammer, 'Economic Anthropology and the Sociology of Development', pp. 223–4.
28. Terray, ibid., pp. 140–1.
29. Ibid., p. 147.
30. Ibid., p. 148.
31. See L. Dumont, *Homo Hierarchicus* (London, 1970) for an interesting viewpoint on the question of hierarchy.
32. G. Godelier, in *Les Temps Modernes*, 1965; Dupré and Rey, 'Reflections on the Pertinence of a Theory of the History of Exchange', p. 151.
33. G. Dupré, and P-P. Rey, 'Théorie de l'histoire des échanges, exemple de l'Ouest Congolais (Congo-Brazzaville)'. Unpublished MS. p. 33, quoted in Terray, p. 167.
34. See, however, B. Hindess and P. Q. Hirst, *Pre-Capitalist Modes of Production* (London, 1975); M. Godelier, 'The Object and Method of Economic Anthropology', in Godelier, 1972, pp. 249–319; P. Winch, *The Idea of a social Science, and its Relation to Philosophy* (London, 1958).
35. In Godelier, ibid.
36. Ibid., pp. 251–7.
37. Ibid., p. 317.
38. T. Asad, 'The Concept of Rationality in Economic Anthropology', *Economy and Society*, vol. 3, no. 2, 1974, p. 213.
39. Godelier, p. viii.

4 Economic Anthropology and the Problems of Development

Complementary to André Gunder Frank's[1] analysis of models of the 'macro-relationships' between Metropoli and their colonial or neo-colonial satellites in the context of the notion of *dependence* and *exploitation*, lies the analysis of the same key notions in terms of, on the one hand, relationships between modes of production within pre- or non-capitalist economic systems, and, on the other, to relationships between such non-capitalist modes and the capitalist mode itself. In turn, the whole discussion revolves around the question of the applicability of economic concepts deriving from capitalism to economic systems whose characteristics are different from, or in opposition to, the capitalist mode.

My project here will be to attempt to throw some light on this second area by way of a critical examination of the largely unknown (certainly to sociologists) and unappreciated literature deriving from the French economic anthropologists who are concerned with this issue, and, in passing beyond the level of a critique, to relate the theoretical importance of this group to the twin issues of the nature of the fundamental conceptual basis of economic anthropology (and therefore of economics), on the one hand, and to the bearing of this on the more classical concerns of the sociology of development, on the other. In so doing, it is to be hoped that we might be both able to supply some theoretical discussion of the 'missing term', which lies between the analysis of the workings of international capitalism at a general level, and the implementation of detailed studies of the operation of these forces at a truly local level in indigenous contexts, and to thereby make some move towards the integration of economic anthropology and

47

the sociology of development, disciplines which are not conceptually, and should not be institutionally, distinct. The wider
purpose must therefore be seen not so much as the transcending of
Frank's seminal work, but as an attempt to give some substantial
theoretical flesh to his often imprecise formulations.

But an understanding of the nature and purpose of the radical
rethinking of the French neo-Marxists must be seen against the
background of the whole Anglo-American tradition in economic
anthropology, for it is from the criticism of this tradition, and in
particular some of its key figures – Firth, Dalton, Bohannan and
Polanyi – together with a return less to Marx himself than to
certain ideas inspired by him, that the positive programmes of the
French radicals emerge. It is to the nature of this Anglo-American
tradition that we must therefore turn.

THE 'LIBERAL' TRADITION

Contemporary economic anthropology has been largely dominated in recent years by the controversy surrounding the validity of
applying concepts derived from 'classical' or conventional
economics to the anthropological sphere. I do not intend to survey
the details of this controversy: this has already been done perfectly
adequately.[2] Instead I propose to examine the principal ideas of
perhaps the single most creative economic anthropologist in
recent history: Raymond Firth. This approach has the additional
advantage of highlighting the main theoretical concerns of
modern economic anthropology, for it is these that Firth has
largely created or addressed himself to.

I will begin my exposition of Firth with the statement of four
propositions which are axiomatic to his whole approach to
economic anthropology.[3] First, there is the distinction between
what is commonly called 'primitive technology' and economic
anthropology proper, defined as an essentially institutional study.
Secondly, there is the suggestion that the conceptual clarifications
achieved by economists of the essential nature of *economic*
problems, particularly where they relate to the behaviour of
people in choice-making situations in the context of the disposal of
available resources, can be imported into the study of economic
anthropology. Thirdly, there is the methodological proposition
that the understanding of the nature of particular social systems
can only be achieved when the nature of the particular economic

system embodied in the social system is itself understood. And finally there is the claim that the divorce from 'primitive technology' and the borrowing of economic concepts has increased the interest in analytical problems to the extent that theory, including the subject's reflection on its own nature, has become a paramount concern of economic anthropologists.

The role of material 'things' is basic to any economy yet it has become increasingly apparent that economics, particularly when applied to small-scale communities, is essentially the study of *relationships*. And the economic anthropologist, because of the nature of his material, is obliged to recognise the reciprocity between forms of social relationship and the movement of material goods. The corollary of this is, of course, the proposition that there is an indissoluble relationship between any social system and its related economic system, such that one cannot be adequately explained or understood without reference to the other. Indeed, this polarity of 'economic' and 'social' becomes more unreal the more one examines it. This may seem self-evident to the economic anthropologist who may be working at a fairly low level of abstraction, but it carries with it the interesting point that, if it is true, the possibility of divorcing social from economic factors becomes less viable at every level, which admits the possibility of systematic error into areas of economic which are tempted to regard the economic system as a self-regulating and abstract scheme of essentially mathematical relationships between abstract entities. Notions such as 'value' and 'demand' are empty unless they are seen in an essentially social context, and the economist must logically admit that if he is willing to import his own high level abstract concepts into economic anthropology, then the contrary must be true. Thus Firth is correct in asserting that while certain economic concepts may or may not seem applicable to economic anthropology, there is no *a priori* way of deciding this: it must be tested empirically in the individual case by the anthropologist who has the data. Firth's debt to Malinowski in arriving at this position of the economic transactions being regarded as acts with a social meaning, rather than as transmissions of objects, is clear even though he diverges on almost all points of detail.[4] There arises from this the second and normative point, that is, the assertion that economic anthropology *should* and indeed *must* be a theoretical and analytic discipline and not simply a descriptive one. Firth's recognition that anthropology is essentially a comparative study makes this

problem acute by calling into question the theoretical basis of the
subject at the two levels of (i) the general applicability of
economic concepts in economic anthropology, and (ii) the
universal applicability of any given concept once it has been tested
and found sound in a particular case.

Firth's general position on this is clear, when speaking of a
particular economic concept he says:

> Evidence of gross difference between primitive, peasant and
> industrial economic systems is obvious. But absence of general
> markets for goods and services of all kinds and the lack of
> impersonal market relationships *does not mean the lack of any
> concept of economic advantage* ... the differences *lie primarily in the
> structural and institutional fields. On the basic principles of choice in the
> use of resources and perception of relative worth in an exchange, there is a
> continuum of behaviour over the whole range of human economic systems.*
> From this point of view it may be argued that the relation
> sometimes postulated as a disjunction between economics and
> anthropology is of the same order as the relation between
> economics and economic history. When the anthropologist or
> historian applies an empirical institutional test to theoretical
> economic propositions, the propositions themselves may be
> found to need amplification or modification by specifying more
> precisely the conditions in which they operate. But anthropo-
> logist no more than historian needs to reject the whole
> apparatus of economic analysis.[5]

Firth's position explicitly then, is that it is possible, on the basis
of the general uniformity of human economic reactions, to employ
the basic approach of economic analysis in primitive contexts,
given that the relationship between primitive system and modern
analysis is a dialogue in which both sides may come to be seen in a
different light. This, I take it, is the reason behind Frankenberg
characterising Firth's position as 'Neo-Classical'.[6] Let us expand
this a little as it is the key to Firth's whole approach.

Firth starts from the assumption that all men in all societies are
faced with the same economic problem: how to allocate scarce
resources between alternative uses, given that some uses are more
highly valued than others. He sees the main task of economic
anthropology to be the study of how men organise their activities
in solving the problem of allocation within the limits set by their

physical environment, as transformed by culture, their technology and state of knowledge, their social structure and values. He denies that men in primitive and peasant societies are mere automata driven by the demands of their environment and social structure, and sees them as exercising choice in having to economise as men do in more complex societies. In analysing this aspect of conduct, anthropologists can use economic categories and economic analysis. Thus while primitive economies lack most of the specialised economic institutions that we associate with industrial societies, these alone need not be the object of economic analysis, and other forms of relationships may equally well be abstracted and examined, such as the processes of how people allocate their time between production of different categories of goods, of how goods and services are distributed and exchanged, how labour is mobilised and utilised and the factors influencing decisions on these matters. These economic relationships function as part of a wider system of social involvements and moral imperatives, which are to be found also in industrial societies: the difference between types of economic systems is one of degree, not kind.

This view has been challenged on the basis that certain *essential* features of economies as we (i.e. western economists) know them are missing from primitive systems. I think that Firth has partly forestalled this criticism by allowing that while, as he explicitly admits in many places, there are vast differences between primitive and modern economies, nevertheless, given that they can withstand the empirical tests for validity, individual economic concepts can be utilised universally, which is *not* what the anti-Firthian economists are arguing about.[7] The failure to resolve this problem seems to stem from an essential lack of communication: the economists who deny the validity of their concepts when applied to primitive cases are denying this possibility on the basis of the greater or lesser lack of certain of these *same* key concepts in the primitive economy in question. What we *should* be arguing about is how far *any* alien concepts can be used to explain a system which does not share the same presuppositions as the culture from which those concepts arise. In the context of this paper I do not wish to enter this question. My point in making it is to demonstrate that the controversy as to whether or not we can employ classical economic concepts is empty until we specify the terms on which to argue.

A resolution of the problem cannot even be attempted on the basis laid down by Frankenberg, Dalton[8] and others. In this context, involving Firth as the 'Neo-classical' protagonist is pointless in that, while he recognises Malinowski's maxim that 'Nothing is so misleading in ethnographic accounts as the description of facts of native civilizations in terms of our own' (*Argonauts*), he is not blindly applying a set of economic points of reference to all economies and hoping for universally valid results. His claim that

> what is required of Economic Anthropology is the analysis of material in such a way that it will be directly comparable with the material of modern economics, matching assumption with assumption and so allowing generalizations to be ultimately framed which will subsume the phenomena of both price and non-price commodities into a body of principles about human behaviour which will be truly universal[9]

is not contrary to the more modest claim that we have characterised Firth as holding earlier when it is remembered that Firth is not claiming that he *has* found such a body of universal principles, but that this is the ideal, the paradigm of what any science should achieve. To argue that he is here misconceiving the nature of the human sciences is one thing and is a quite different issue altogether from arguing that he has contradicted his more moderate position.

This is not, however, to deny the absence of problems. It is indeed true, for instance, that Firth's work contains no reference to the problems of dependence and exploitation, nor in any serious way (until very recently) to traditions of economic thought which lie outside classical capitalism. Simply to plead empiricism is clearly not enough – this is largely what the epistemologies of Structuralism and Marxism have struggled against. Similarly, the misleading and theoretically inadequate 'underlabourer' conception of economic anthropology – the 'filling the gaps in the economist's data' – exists in Firth's view of the subject in large measure. Equally, the view that, 'where the economic anthropologist is still uncertain of his role is in the degree to which he should or can raise to a more abstract level the propositions he derives from the data he empirically gathers' is just a function of the present state of knowledge, is naïve in the extreme.

In the light of this we must begin anew. Many of the arguments of Dalton, Polanyi, Sahlins, Burling and Herskovits[10] may simply be misconceiving the nature of the problem. Few would wish to argue that the precise conceptual vocabulary of theoretical economics can be introduced *in toto* and without modification into economic anthropology. In practice, the process is much more *ad hoc* than this, as Barth, Paine[11] and others have shown. To begin afresh we must recognise (a) what is to be meant by 'economic analysis', (b) the characteristics of the societies being studied by the economic anthropologist, and (c) the limitations of concepts from any other discipline when applied to anthropology. Anthropologists, while correctly recognising that much can be learnt from other disciplines, have undoubtedly leaned far too heavily on the concepts that those subjects have developed for themselves. Economic anthropology, perhaps more than most other specialised sub-branches of the activity, must develop its own concepts appropriate to its own peculiar needs.

THE FRENCH CRITIQUE

It is in response to these problems that a wide-ranging critique of 'liberal' economic anthropology has arisen in France, drawing its inspiration from Marx largely by way of Althusser. While not recognising themselves as composing a 'school' in the narrow sense, the common presuppositions, interests and purposes of the anthropologists I shall examine are so closely related that they may, nevertheless, be called by this term. The use of Althusserian language, aspects of his methodology, the common interest in Marx's mature works (and in particular *Capital*), as opposed to his early ones, and the extension of certain Althusserian preoccupations (and in particular that of modes of production) equally allows us to identify something stronger than a mere tendency. In this sense also the movement is a neo-Marxist one, rather than a 'classical' one, as I will attempt to make clearer. I will thus proceed by examining in some detail the contribution of Dupré and Rey[12] and Claude Meillassoux[13] to this debate, for it is in the works of these that the clearest exposition is to be found. Other and less central contributors (for example E. Terray,[14] M. Godelier[15] and Coquery-Vidrovich[16]) will be referred to only where a clear link with my central exposition (and subsequent critique) can be seen to exist.

Dupré and Rey's discussion (like that of Meillassoux's of 1972) begins with the rejection of the classification and interpretation of economic systems based exclusively on *forms of exchange*, and in particular of the models presented by Bohannan and Dalton[17] and Polanyi,[18] and in the bringing into opposition with this a Marxian analysis of the relationships between capitalist and 'traditional' modes of production and of the 'theory of the reproduction' of such formations. The details of the internal critique of Bohannan and Dalton and Polanyi I will leave to one side, and attempt to draw out only those aspects of the discussion concerned directly with Dupré and Rey's opposition to liberal economics as obscuring the true nature of dependence and exploitation.

What has to be explained is the historical problem that in many instances economic 'change' (or 'development') exerts its influence over 'traditional' economies by impelling them from being 'marketless economies', through the stage of being 'economies with peripheral markets' to their economic climax, 'economies in which the Market Principle is dominant'. But the real question is whether such a progression is to be explained by a liberal ('idealist') model which sees the seeds of the 'market principle' which comes to penetrate the entire society in pre-market institutions (whether in African societies, or in the Classical World, as with Polanyi) and which 'develops by means of its own forces, independently of any other structure than that of exchange', or by an historical one which 'does not conceal the fact that the famous "market principle" only developed through the coloniser's violent intervention against the previous mode of production'. What is needed therefore is a method which can take account of this in a concrete way – a method possessing 'theoretical unity', rather than one which operates through the fake oppositions of liberal economics, and particularly one which repudiates the view that market and non-market economies stand in a relationship of 'reciprocal exclusion', i.e. that 'the market system and other systems are absolutely incompatible'. Equally such a method must combat the insidious belief that 'from the moment the market is introduced the hitherto anthropological analysis gives way to the principles of liberal economics'.

The demonstration of this thesis involves Dupré and Rey in two linked expositions: one is the 'role of exchange in the reproduction of the conditions of production' in lineage societies; the other is the argument that

> Almost in the centre of each particular system the place of exchange in the articulation of these systems will be justified by its role in the process of one system's domination of another, and this role will be determined in the last instance by the dominant mode of production.[19]

The former exposition, of which I will try and point out the essence (and some of its equally essential difficulties), is based upon an analysis by Meillassoux[20] of the significance of exchange between the elders of lineage groups. Meillassoux quite rightly identifies the fact that the control that the elders possess over the goods produced in a lineage cannot be explained by reference to their powers of physical coercion, which they do not have, or by reference to their control of technical knowledge, over which they have no monopoly, nor by reference to their kinship relations, which are only the expression of, and not the basis for, social cohesion. On the contrary, their power is based on the twin abilities to 'reserve for themselves control of social knowledge' (genealogies, marriage regulations, etc.) and the corollary of this, 'the spheres of artifice' (magic, divination etc.) on the one hand, and on the other

> Above all, they reserve for themselves control of the cadets' and their own access to women, and they guarantee this control by holding the 'elite goods' which are indispensable for marriage. This last weapon of the elders has an original character compared with the weapons considered above: it is that whereas all the others were *individual weapons* of each particular elder within his particular group, this is a *collective weapon* belonging to all *the elders of the* different lineage groups.[21]

In detail then, the elders maintain control of the material aspects of matrimonial exchanges, they thereby 'guarantee the control of the demographic reproduction of the lineages', and in addition they retain control over the exchange of slaves, thereby controlling also the 'redistribution of men from demographically strong lineages towards demographically weak ones'.

It is, according to the argument, this demographic reproduction which is the leading condition for, in lineage societies, the reproduction of the conditions of production. This contrasts with Marx's 'ancient societies' where this reproduction must be sought in the 'defence or acquisition of land, preservation of the global liberty of the community or enslavement of the defeated community'. Social structure can also be accounted for in that 'control of the reproduction of the technical conditions of production (unit of labour demographically adapted) guarantees the reproduction of the social relations (dependence of the cadets with respect to the elders)'.

It might well be asked what has happened to the notions of dependence and exploitation in the course of all this? The very existence of a relation of dependence suggests to Dupré and Rey that exploitation, something not normally associated with 'lineage' societies, may in fact exist in such typically 'anthropological' societies, provided that an adequate definition of exploitation is employed. To show that this is the case involves a rejection of Godelier's definition that 'Exploitation begins when appropriation of the surplus is effected without conterpart',[22] on the grounds that this suggests that exploitation would not really occur in any kind of society, and that it also implies that

> capitalists exploit less in so far as they provide a more significant counterpart, that is, in so far as they consign a greater part of the surplus product to the development of the forces of production and a lesser part to their personal consumption,[23]

a position antithetical to that of Marx. The true answer indeed should be sought in Marx's early view that exploitation occurs when the product turns against the producer and increases his subjection.

> We propose the following definition of the concept: exploitation exists when the use of the surplus product by a group (or an aggregate) which has not contributed the corresponding surplus of labour reproduces the conditions of a new extortion or surplus labour from the producers.[24]

Exploitation, then, is a notion with a potential range of application extending far beyond the conventional boundaries of capitalism.

From the recognition of this to an application of the definition to the relationship between 'traditional' modes of production and the capitalist one is an obvious step (as least in so far as the historical contact between colonial capitalism and lineage social formations is concerned). This contact is seen by Dupré and Rey as falling into three phases: (i) the period of slave trade when 'the European market economy got its supplies essentially by playing on the internal contradictions of the lineage social formations'; (ii) a transitional phase, that of 'colonialism proper' which is 'characterized by ambiguity: it is a matter of using the economic basis characteristic of lineage society to establish the conditions of transition to capitalism'; and (iii) 'At the end of this process a new type of social formation is to be constituted where the capitalist mode of production is dominant; and with capitalism once established, it is to be dominated by the capitalism of the metropolitan country, that is, to depend on it for its reproduction: this is neo-colonialism.'[25] It must be noted, however, that Dupré and Rey's claim, that 'in each of the systems (capitalist and lineage) *exchange* plays a dominant role in the reproduction of one of these systems over another system with which it is articulated',[26] is based on some measure of semantic confusion, involving as it does the belief that the term has the same application in all its uses and in relation to all kinds of economic systems, even to the extent of assimilating the notion of a *medium of exchange* to their unitary model, a move which brings them perilously close to the logic of the vilified Dalton/Bohannan/Polanyi position, despite disclaimers to the contrary.[27] The relationship between systems of exchange and the transition from one mode of production to another stand in need of considerable clarification (of which more below) even assuming that (contra Meillassoux) the transition is ever a complete one, an assumption not supported by history, as the authors agree.[28] In the conclusion to their paper Dupré and Rey summarise and expand their 'phase' characterisation of the encroachment of capitalist domination over traditional modes of production, and draw attention to the fact that several modes of production can co-exist simultaneously in a colonial or neo-colonial context. In so doing they place themselves in a close relationship with Meillassoux who is in large measure concerned with the expansion of this latter point. (The internal connections between Meillassoux's and Dupré and Rey's theoretical positions are numerous and I will point them out where they are relevant.)

Meillassoux's contribution to the present debate is to be found mainly in three papers which draw heavily upon the material presented in his notable book in the field of African economic anthropology. The essence of his theoretical position may be found in the two later papers (1972, 1974) and it is upon these that I will concentrate.

The importance of Meillassoux should not, however, be traced to his generalised, patriarchal and neo-evolutionist and, curiously enough, in terms of its ethnographic basis, highly particular and localised, general theory,[29] but to the insights contained at the end of his 1972 paper and developed in his 1974 one. In essence these relate to the claim that 'agricultural self-sustaining formations' (*'sociétés traditionnelles d'auto-subsistance'*) contain within themselves all the necessary means of coping with the basic social, economic and other needs of their members. The grafting on to them of production for external markets can only bring about their transformation into class societies, or it will fail, or such communities are (or should be) dissolved and replaced by a new type of unit. However,

> Paradoxically, the capitalist exploiters, who are often better Marxists than Marxist theoreticians, are aware of the potentiality of this contradictory situation. The agricultural self-sustaining communities, because of their comprehensiveness and their *raison d'etre* are able to fulfil functions that capitalism prefers not to assume in the under-developed countries: the functions of social security. The cheap cost of labour in these countries comes from the super-exploitation, not only of the labour from the wage-earner himself but also of the labour of his kin group.[30]

In other words movements between the urban capitalist sector and the rural 'traditional' one in, for instance, South Africa, is to be explained not by psychology or demography, but by reference to the economic fact that people who are obliged to become wage-labourers in a neo- or quasi-colonial situation are forced back on the 'traditional' sector to obtain precisely those services which the capitalist does not provide – sickness, unemployment and old age benefits. Much of the so-called 'dual economy' theory is thus to be seen as an attempt to conceal the exploitation of the rural community, integrated ... as an organic component of capitalist production to feed the temporarily unproductive workers of the capitalist sector and supply them with the resources necessary to their survival. Because of this process of absorption within the capitalist economy, the agricultural communities, maintained as reserves of cheap labour, are being undermined and perpetuated at the same time, undergoing a prolonged crisis and not a smooth transition to capitalism.[31]

Equally, the pool of labour power itself is reproduced in the 'traditional' context and then drawn off into the capitalist sector. The two 'spheres' of the economy thus stand in and perpetuate with respect to each other a relation of exploitation, inequality and dependence.[32]

The situation in practice is not a static one. For, on the one hand, the capitalist system must avoid a *direct* intrusion of capital into the traditional sector, if that sector is to continue unchanged, a restraint that capitalism rarely finds it possible to sustain. (In this later paper (1974) Meillassoux continues to use the term 'self-sustaining' sector, a term not really applicable after the advent of capitalism/colonialism.) Equally, on the other hand, attempts to 'fix' the traditional system, to confine it to some unchanging pattern, are similarly doomed to failure, for without the equally traditional means of outlet – territorial expansion, means of demographic control and avenues of creativity – the 'native' sector is set on the road to sterility and impoverishment. Contradictions *within* and *between* the spheres of a 'dual' economy are thus closely and internally linked.

CRITIQUE

There are some severe difficulties, both logical and empirical, with these theses which I will briefly indicate. In the first place, Dupré and Rey's argument is a systematic perpetration of the sin of Africocentrism: the belief widespread in England and apparently also in France, that African societies and their institutions exhaust all that there is of theoretical or empirical interest in anthropology. Many of the failings of the argument stem from adopting this position, and then in not pursuing it with complete single-mindedness and thereby failing to take note of counter-evidence from other parts of the same continent. The logical and empirical difficulties are equally so closely related that I will not attempt to examine them separately.

The first point to establish is a general conceptual one – that Dupré and Rey nowhere define the key notion of 'mode of production' and consequently succeed in making it a very flexible stick with which to beat the 'liberals'. More particularly, the inner connections between a mode of production and its corresponding system of distribution (the latter the classical concern of the liberals, according also to Meillassoux) are left to one side, and more significantly, so is any discussion of the very tenable argument that a 'mode of production' (logically) contains the means of its own reproduction: this is *part of its definition*. Instead, distribution and exchange are confused, the latter is reduced to *explaining* the 'reproduction of the conditions of production' and the whole is assimilated to a highly dubious (and highly generalised) theory of elder dominance within and between 'lineage societies'.

The dubiousness of this theory derives from its premises which can be summarised as follows, (and seen to be dubious as soon as they are clearly stated): (i) goods produced by the 'cadets' are entirely controlled by the elders; (ii) that 'social knowledge' is exclusively in the hands of the elders, while 'technical knowledge' is not (even if such a distinction is valid); (iii) that the elders conspire amongst themselves and between lineages to retain this exclusive knowledge; (iv) that thereby they control demographic reproduction (there is confusion between various uses of the terms 'reproduction' and about the relationships between demography and kinship: the elders control *matrimonial exchanges*); (v) that they thereby control the reproduction of the lineages ; (vi) that (contrary to Meillassoux's original formulation) the elders do possess powers of physical coercion whereby they can reduce a cadet to slavery; (vii) that, unlike in 'ancient societies', relationships between lineages are *not* based on warfare or conceptions of property or territoriality, but on the 'exchange' and 'conspiracy' functions between elders ('conflict takes place in a field deter-mined externally by exchange between the elders'[33]); (viii) it is assumed that the relationship between 'economy' and 'social structure' is a relatively simple one, mediated by the concept of 'control of reproduction of the technical conditions of production' (which in turn involves a 'power' or hierarchy model of social relations where the Dupré/Rey/Meillassoux argument is to hold); and finally (ix) that the claim that 'demographic reproduction appears to be the essential condition for the reproduction of the conditions of production in lineage society'[34] is something more than the tautology and truism that it appears to be. The theory is additionally not an historical one: it has to do only with the *maintenance* of 'dependence' and not with its *establishment*, a claim which embodies a view of the relationship between 'structure' and 'history' of dubious utility to a Marxian.

Our criticisms of Meillassoux's position specifically fall into an additional set of categories. In the course of his 1972 paper, his argument leads him into a critique of liberal economics directed against the belief that, stemming from the alleged universality of the 'laws' of capitalism, non-capitalist economies are simply underdeveloped forms of capitalism, and that therefore the methods of liberal economics apply equally to all kinds of economic formations. This in turn involves an attack on certain key 'liberals', and in particular Sahlins and Raymond Firth, which does little justice to the range and complexity of the thought of either of those writers or the real nature of their positive contributions to economic anthropology, and commits such elementar errors as castigating Firth for not distinguishing use-value from exchange-value, or for only dimly perceiving the 'possible influence of social situation on behaviour instead of the reverse'.[35] Such claims cannot be justified, and can only be partly excused if seen as overstatements for the purpose of highlighting an allegedly contrary view held by Meillassoux. This is supported by the claim that 'all liberal economic anthropology is centred on problems of distribution and never on those of production'.[36] While this is undoubtedly true, the existence of a logical connection between production and distribution is never seen by Meillassoux as a factor determining the whole way in which the 'problematic' of economic anthropology must be phrased. Related to this is the belief that the approach to pre-capitalist (Meillassoux uses the prefix *pre* without qualms) formation pioneered by Marx in the 'Pre-capitalist Economic Formations' should be abandoned in favour of the method of *Capital*.[37] The full implications of this are not elaborated upon. Meillassoux's claim, therefore, is that we should concentrate on 'the social organization of production: who is working with whom and for whom? Where does the product of the labourer go? Who controls the product? How does the economic system reproduce itself?'[38]

Meillassoux's discussion of Marx's distinction between land as a 'subject of labour' and as an 'instrument of labour' then leads him into a two part theory. (1) The distinction between hunting/gathering and agricultural societies, based on certain false and Africocentric assumptions that:

> The hunters, once they share the common product, are free from any reciprocal obligations or allegiance. The process gives no ground for the emergence of a social hierarchy or of a centralized power, or even the extended family organization. The basic social unit is an equalitarian but unstable band with little concern for biological or social reproduction.[39]

This can only be seen as a wilfully negligent misinterpretation of known ethnographic facts. (2) An argument (and it is not clear if the argument is offered as a model or an empirical generalisation) of 'elder domination' closely related to that of Dupré and Rey, but largely confined to relations of production *within* the 'agricultural community' and which somewhat modifies their conception of the role of exchange:

> These relations of production are materialized through a redistributive system of circulation. ... This is not a system of exchange, properly speaking, since the products are never offered for each other and therefore not subjected to the appraisal of their respective value. It is rather a continuously renewed cycle of *advance* and *restitution* of subsistence.

The other major divergence lies in Meillassoux's seeing the elders as *directly* determining this cycle of subsistence by receiving and managing the produce of the 'cadets' and in turn advancing them food and seed. So, in turn, 'Control over subsistence is not control of the means of production but of the means of physiological *reproduction*, used to reproduce the life of the human producer.'[40]

In other words, the leaders of such societies 'rely less on the control of the *means of material production* than on the *means of human reproduction*: subsistence and women.'[41] The assimilation of 'subsistence' to the category of 'reproduction' is significant, but leaves very unclear the exact rationale for creating an (artificial?) distinction in 'agricultural societies' between subsistence and 'means of material production'. Additionally as Gledhill puts it:

> One of the most striking features of 'primitive economic organisation' is the way in which competition for status is often kept sharply separate from the question of the organisation of society at the 'subsistence' level. Restrictions on the convertibility of goods between spheres, restrictions on the alienation of property, most notably land and one's own person, the principle of redistribution and the specification of rights of access to the means of production, all these conditions control distribution within the substantive economic infrastructure, whilst scarcity and competition – one might borrow Lévi-Strauss' use of the term 'entropy' here – are restricted to a secondary level of activity and circulation.[42]

The control of women and matrimonial policy is again the key to this. The same criticisms brought against Dupré and Rey apply equally (and perhaps more so – his model is cruder) to Meillassoux's theory of patriarchy.

TOWARDS A BROADER THEORY

The whole of the foregoing analysis has directed attention to some (and only some) aspects of the relationship between colonial or neo-colonial capitalism and local economies and social structures, and in particular as this relates to the concepts of 'structrual dependency' and 'exploitation'. There are certain obvious gaps, especially in Meillassoux's argument, amongst which might be included any analysis of *commodity extracting* exploitation as opposed to *labour power extracting* exploitation, and the question of how far certain kinds of relations of *dependency* necessarily imply relations of *exploitation* and the development of links between all these things and indigenous social structures. Similarly, one finds parallel inadequacies in Frank's analysis when it comes to the question of the *exact* nature of the articulation (or rather disarticulation) between the urban–industrial and rural–peasant sectors in underdeveloped countries. The famous Frankian metaphor of a 'chain' of metropolitan-satellite relationships stretching from the world centres of capitalism to the most isolated peasant[43] needs a corresponding clarification. Many of the ways in which this clarification might be achieved are suggested by the 'French School's' approach. For instance, the *co-existence* of several modes of production, including traditional with capitalist modes, and the implications of this in terms of their articulation must be incorporated into a 'metropolis-satellite' model. The significance of the seemingly purely internal anthropological debate on the subject of markets thus reappears in a new light when seen in this context. In other words, the question of the nature of exchanges between sectors reasserts itself, and in so doing points again to the logically necessary internal connection between production and distribution, and once again underlines the analytical vacuousness of concentrating upon 'modes of production' to, at the worst exclusion of, and at the best trivialisation of, systems of distribution. Indeed, we must turn to the fundamental question of the definition of 'mode of production', and of its utility as an analytical tool once defined.

Terray, in opening his analysis of Meillassoux's *Anthropologie Économique des Gouro de Côte d'Ivoire*, starts from a criticism of the narrow definition of 'mode of production' employed in that work. This criticism has two aspects – that to reduce the concept of a mode of production to 'the enunciation of a few general characteristics of "self-subsistence economies" is ... a waste of its operational fruitfulness', and that the implication that all such societies have the *same* mode of production excludes the attempt 'to explain the great variety of social and ideological relations observed in such societies'.[44] The point behind this is that, according to Marx, a simple description of an economy does not exhaust the concept of 'mode of production'. (A point also obscured by Meillassoux in his 1972 paper when he simply remarks, 'Recognition of various economic formations comes generally from the observation of different "ways of living", such as hunting, cultivating, cattle herding, etc., which must not be confused with modes of production, *though they may coincide with the latter*').[45] Meillassoux's confusion is essentially that he restricts 'mode of production' to the *productive activities* themselves (the process of appropriation), thus excluding not only the juridico-political and ideological superstructures, but even the *relations of production*, all of which he then has to reintegrate into his analysis. (His production/distribution dichotomy can also be seen as stemming from this.) In fact, as Terray, following Etienne Balibar, points out, 'productive forces and relations of production do not relate to two separate categories of "things" but are two aspects of one single "reality"'[46] (i.e. the economic base of a mode of production). And as he goes on

> these same factors are involved in definite social relations which constitute the structure of the process of production, seen as the social appropriation of the product. Here we find relations of production which allocate the agents and means of production, and the division of the product which follows that allocation.[47]

And again, 'Thus a study of relations of production is only possible through the enumeration and examination of relations of distribution.'

A mode of production in its most limited sense, therefore, is something more than a description of the process of appropriation, for it must encompass both the forces of production and the social relations of production. Two principal issues arise from this. First, there is the claim that we can undoubtedly establish that while it is legitimate to function with more than one operational definition of 'mode of production', the usage in question *must be defined* in each case, and precisely what the implications of the usage chosen are must be indicated. Many of Meillassoux's difficulties stem from a lack of awareness of the range of his concepts. The Althusserian use of the term 'mode of production' is an instance of this, where not only is the concept extended beyond its limited usage, but exists specifically within the context of a particular kind of structural analysis.[48] Secondly, there is the question of what happens when we go looking for modes of production, and the suggested answer, that we always find more than one in a combination of one dominant and the other(s) subordinate, the articulation of the relationship between them resulting in the concrete social formation under examination.

By a circuitous route we have thus arrived back at our central theme as originally posed (in practice, of course, all these 'subsidiary' issues are tied to it). The expansion of his argument indeed leads Terray into a vigorous defence of Meillassoux against Dupré and Rey and their 'discovery' of exploitation and class antagonisms in lineage societies, and their belief that evidence for this can be found in Meillassoux's own writings. This defence is partly based on an empirical argument, that their conception of chiefly office is incorrect in that they do not see that 'The elder plays the same part in matrimonial exchanges as he does in material production: in both cases his power is simply a function of his office.' In other words

> To put it more generally, Rey and Dupré see the moment of tribute as determinant in the cycle of tributes and redistributions: the elder monopolizes the product of the labour of the juniors and hence presides over the redistribution. On the contrary, to me the moment of redistribution comes first and the moment of tribute is only its necessary consequence.[49]

But the defence is also based on the belief that in committing this error of partiality it leads him to assimilate their position to bourgeois economics:

> Pierre-Philippe Rey and Georges Dupré did not consider the process of reproduction as a whole, but only at the *single moment of circulation*: it may be this that led them to see the relations between elder and junior as between exploiter and exploited. The errors into which this attitude has led bourgeois political economy are common knowledge ... The ethnologist ratifies this 'representation' when he isolates the moment of circulation in the process of reproduction: like the bourgeois economist he then asks himself whether the relations of circulation are the site of an equilibrium or an antagonism and his answer will depend on whether he favors a static or a dynamic ethnology.[50]

While warmly agreeing with Terray's criticism of Dupré and Rey, it must not be forgotten that very similar points can in fact be made against Meillassoux himself (although not necessarily against the *Anthropologie Economique des Gouro*). We should also retain some awareness of the general anthropological principles lying behind the notions of 'surplus' and 'distribution':

> The idea of surplus is still obscured by the notion that many people still hold that there is a necessary causality between the existence of a surplus and that of the exploitation of man by man. This raises the general problem not of the mechanisms,

but of the 'principles' of distribution, since the latter can be either equal or unequal among the members of a society. One and the same society may, moreover, follow different principles; depending on the objects which are to be distributed. The Siane ensure equal access for everyone to the use of land and to subsistence foodstuffs. Luxury goods, however, such as tobacco and salt, depend on the initiative of each individual. As for actual wealth – feathers, shells, pigs – the material basis for ceremonial acts and for access to women, these are controlled by the elders of the families and the important men (*bosboi*), whose prestige and power they symbolize. But this inequality does not signify at all that there is exploitation of some by others.[51]

The broader theory towards which we are working will thus involve the making clear of a number of distinctions. Some of these are obviously conceptual ones – the problem of the definition of 'mode of production', the identification of such modes, their articulation and their relationship to other aspects of the social formations in question. Related to this will be the notion of 'exploitation' in non-capitalist contexts and the links between 'exploitation' and 'dependence' when non-capitalist societies come into contact with capitalist ones. Also closely associated with this is the question of where social classes enter the arena, and at what point a class analysis becomes possible. The importance of conceptual clarity is thus of primary importance both within economic anthropology, and as economic anthropology bears upon the expansion of the Frankian model. The broadening of the vocabulary of anthropology also results from this. Anthropology as a whole has very successfully (to date) insulated itself from the conceptual repertoire not only of sociology, but of Marxism as well.

A second group of distinctions emerges from this. The distinction between *types* of relationships between capitalism and its subject peoples are rarely made clear from within the 'macroperspective' of the sociology of development. In the light of the foregoing discussion we can see that significant differences exist between (a) settler colonisation and the *destruction* of indigenous societies, (b) surplus expropriation colonisation where material wealth is removed and (c) labour expropriation, where the native population is essential and has to be preserved.

The relationships between colonial or neo-colonial capitalism and indigenous social structures will vary correspondingly. Thus not only Frank but also Baran with his theory of the *decomposition* of pre-capitalist structure need modification.[52]

A third group of issues involve anthropology itself in a clarification of some of its most basic and classical preoccupations in the light of the present debate. At the level of practice the uncovering of the *horizontal* as well as the *vertical* linkages that exist in all social situations is clearly an aspect of this. At the level of theory we must reject the 'under-labourer' conception of anthropology, providing the cultural flesh for the planning or 'development' economists' bones,[53] and argue instead that it has a key role in not only illuminating some of the darker areas of the theories of the sociology of development, but in establishing the very basis upon which such theories are constructed. In this respect the classical problems of the 'location' of the economy in the wider social system, the arresting issue (for an economist!) of the 'surplusless economy',[54] the relevance of economic theory nurtured in a capitalist system for societies of an entirely different form of organisation (and, of course, the relevance of that theory for explaining behaviour *within* a putatively capitalist system) all assert their importance. If the wall between economics and epistemology starts to get dangerously thin at this point, this is only to be expected. The general point that should at all costs be established is that the link between the hitherto isolated theoretical concerns of economic anthropology not only should not be, but cannot be divorced from the concerns of a critical sociology of development. Indeed, an anthropologist's discussion of the concept of 'development', which should perhaps have stood at the head of this essay, rather than be implied throughout, is a case in point.

NOTES AND REFERENCES

(Note: all textual citations will be to the English language editions of the works in question where they exist.)

1. A. G. Frank, *Capitalism and Underdevelopment in Latin America* (New York: Monthly Review Press, 1969).
2. R. Frankenberg, 'Economic Anthropology', and P. S. Cohen, 'Economic Analysis and Economic Man', in R. Firth (ed.), *Themes in Economic Anthropology*, ASA Monograph 6 (London, 1967).

3. For references see R. Firth, *Economics of the New Zealand Maori* (Wellington, 1959) pp. 25–6; and R. Firth (ed.), *Themes in Economic Anthropology*, pp. 1–28.
4. Firth, *Themes in Economic Anthropology*, p. 11; and R. Firth, 'The Place of Malinowski in the History of Economic Anthropology', in R. Firth (ed.), *Man and Culture: An Evaluation of the Work of Bronislaw Malinowski* (London, 1957).
5. Firth, *Themes in Economic Anthropology*, p. 6.
6. Frankenberg, 'Economic Anthropology', p. 57.
7. R. Firth, *Primitive Polynesian Economy* (London, 1939), pp. 347 ff.
8. G. Dalton, 'Theoretical Issues in Economic Anthropology', *Current Anthropology*, February, 1969; also G. Dalton, 'Economic Theory and Primitive Society', *American Anthropologist*, 63, 1961.
9. Dalton, quoting *Primitive Polynesian Economy*.
10. K. Polanyi, *Origin of our Time: The Great Transformation* (London, 1946); and K. Polanyi, C. W. Arensberg, H. W. Pearson, *Trade and Market in the Early Empires* (Glencoe, 1957); M. D. Sahlins, 'Political Power and the Economy in Primitive Society', in G. E. Dole and R. L. Carneiro (eds), *Essays in the Science of Culture* (New York, 1960); R. Burling, 'Maximization theories and the study of economic anthropology', *American Anthropologist*, 64, 1962; M. J. Herskovits, *Economic Anthropology* (New York, 1952).
11. F. Barth, *The Role of the Entrepreneur in Social Change in Northern Norway* (Bergen, Oslo, 1963); R. Paine, 'Entrepreneurial Activity Without its Profits', in Ibid.
12. Georges Dupré and Pierre-Philippe Rey, 'Reflections on the Pertinence of a Theory of the History of Exchange', *Economy and Society*, vol. 2, no. 2, 1973. In French, in *Cahiers Internationaux de Sociologie*, vol. 46, 1968.
13. C. Meillassoux, *L'Anthropologie Économique des Gouro de Côte d'Ivoire* (Paris: Mouton, 1964); 'From Reproduction to Production', *Economy and Society*, vol. 1, no. 1, 1972; 'Imperialism as a Mode of Reproduction of Labour Power', (unpublished; forthcoming in *Economy and Society*); 'Essai d'interprétation du phénomène économique dans les sociétés traditionnelles d'auto-subsistence', *Cahiers d'Etudes Africaines*, 4, 1960.
14. E. Terrary, *Marxism and 'Primitive' Societies* (London and New York: Montly Review Press, 1972). In French, *Le Marxisme devant les sociétiés primitives: deux études* (Paris: Maspero, 1969).
15. M. Godelier, *Rationality and Irrationality in Economics* (London: New Left Books, 1972). In French, *Rationalité et irrationalité en économie* (Paris: Maspero, 1966).
16. C. Coquery-Vidrovich whose paper in *Cahiers d'Etudes Africaines*, no. 29, 1968, provides a good deal of Dupré and Rey's background material.
17. P. Bohannan and G. Dalton (eds), *Markets in Africa* (Chicago: Northwestern University Press, 1962).
18. K. Polanyi, C. M. Arensberg and H. W. Pearson (eds), *Trade and Market in the Early Empires* (New York: The Free Press, 1957).
19. Dupré and Rey, 'Reflections on the Pertinence of a Theory of the History of Exchange', p. 144.
20. Meillassoux, 1960 and 1972.
21. Dupré and Rey, 'Reflections on the Pertinence of a Theory of the History of Exchange', p. 145.

70   *Political Economy and the Study of Development*

22. M. Godelier in *Les temps modernes*, vol. 20, 1965.
23. Dupré and Rey, 'Reflections on the Pertinence of a Theory of the History of Exchange' p. 151.
24. Ibid., p. 152.
25. Ibid., pp. 156–7.
26. Ibid., p. 158. My italics.
27. Ibid., pp. 159–60.
28. Ibid., p. 162.
29. E.g., Meillassoux, 1972, especially pp. 98–101.
30. Ibid., p. 102.
31. Ibid., p. 105.
32. Meillassoux, 1974.
33. Dupré and Rey, 'Reflections on the Pertinence of a Theory of the History of Exchange', p. 148.
34. Ibid., p. 147.
35. Meillassoux, 1972, p. 95.
36. Ibid., p. 95.
37. Ibid., p. 98.
38. Ibid., p. 98.
39. Ibid., p. 99.
40. Ibid., p. 100.
41. Ibid., p. 101.
42. J. Gledhill, 'Economics and the theory of games in social anthropology', *Journal of the Anthropological Society of Oxford*, vol. 2, no. 2, 1971, p. 67.
43. A. G. Frank, *Capitalism and Underdevelopment in Latin America*, p. 17.
44. Terray, *Marxism and 'Primitive' Societies*, p. 97.
45. Meillassoux, 1972, p. 98. My italics.
46. Terray, *Marxism and 'Primitive' Societies*, p. 98.
47. Ibid., p. 98.
48. L. Althusser and E. Balibar, *Reading Capital* (London: New Left Books, 1970).
49. Terray, *Marxism and 'Primitive' Societies*, pp. 175–6.
50. Ibid., pp. 173–4. My italics.
51. Godelier, *Rationality and Irrationality in Economics*, p. 275.
52. P. Baran, *The Political Economy of Growth* (London: Calder, 1957).
53. M. Edel, 'Economic Analysis in an Anthropological Setting', *American Anthropologist*, vol. 71, no. 3, 1969.
54. H. W. Pearson, 'The Economy Has No Surplus: A Critique of a Theory of Development', in K. Polanyi *et al.* (eds), *Trade and Market in the Early Empires*.

Part II
The Neo-Marxist Challenge and Renewal

5 Marxism and Anthropology: Reflections and Questions

PREFATORY COMMENTS

The question of Marxian theory in relationship to the non-western world must inevitably raise the parallel question of the status of anthropology. Anthropology, whether seen as the child of the Enlightenment or of Imperialism, is undoubtedly the child of the West. For all its claims to be a 'Science of Man', it has historically been the study by the representatives of the Euro-American culture of Asian, African and indigenous American peoples: the study by a 'subject' of 'objects'. The way out of this vicious circle of intellectual exploitation (which is what it so often becomes) has been suggested by the development of a Marxist anthropology, which radically confronts the questions of colonialism, of the object of anthropological study, of change: which confronts conventional anthropology with a basic challenge by raising again the very question of the nature, theoretical foundations and moral purposes of the discipline itself. This is not to say that the problems are yet solved by Marxist anthropology: indeed they are as yet barely defined. This brief contribution attempts modestly to advance this project by summarising what it sees as being the main issues and putting to Marxist anthropology, or on its behalf, a series of questions which begin to clarify the question of: where next? The successful elaboration of a new problematic certainly suggests new and fruitful approaches for a Marxian perspective on the non-western world which breaks away from the traditional issues which have hitherto dominated this field.

Undoubtedly one of the major movements in anthropology over the last two decades has been the intensive dialogue between 'conventional' social anthropology and Marxism. A stream of

73

monographs, collections, essays, reviews and dissertations has
marked the passage of this debate: a debate which in one sense
has achieved one of the classical signs of having come of age –
people are now looking back, surveying and stocktaking. This
brief paper is not such a stocktaking – rather it is a looking
forward, a posing of a set of questions, an identification of still
murky areas in this complex relationship between Marxism and
anthropology (although it in part arises as a response to one of the
stocktaking enterprises: J. S. Kahn and J. R. Llobera, 'Towards a
New Marxism or a New Anthropology?' in their edited volume
(itself a stocktaking) *The Anthropology of Pre-Capitalist Societies*,
London: Macmillan, 1981). My contention is certainly that this
debate has thrown up at least as many questions as answers –
probably rather more in fact: in the nearly twenty years since C.
Meillassoux published his *Anthropologie Économique des Gouro de
Côte d'Ivoire* (Paris: Mouton, 1964) which many commentatators
see as the seminal work which triggered the whole discussion. My
intention is essentially to indicate what I think those questions
are, and to address them back to the Marxist anthropologists as a
mirror, in which can perhaps be seen both the things done and the
things still to be done.

Curiously, the starting point must really be the question of to
what extent the debate has involved *Marx* at all? Ideas *derivative*
from the work of Marx himself are there in abundance, together
with the occasional pious quotation or citation in a footnote, but
rarely does the master himself appear. Amongst the French
anthropologists for example one finds far more citations from
Althusser than from Marx. To a great extent the 'new anthropology' is *inspired* by Marx's ideas, but to what extent is it actually
Marxist? The source of this problem is twofold: the lack of
cohesion and agreement amongst those claiming in some sense to
be Marxists, on the one hand, and the lack of clear criteria for
exactly what constitutes Marxism, on the other. One has even
read that what makes one a Marxist is the adherence to the
doctrine that in the last analysis the economy is determinant. If
that is all then many of the bourgeoise are certainly Marxists in
their behaviour! There are thus actually two closely related
problems here: that of exactly what constitutes 'Marxism' or
allows one to claim to be or to ascribe to others the label of
Marxist, and that of the extent to which the ideas of Marx himself,
and especially as defined in the 'rigorous' period succeeding the

alleged 'epistemological break' identified by Althusser in the evolution of Marx's writings. Those works of the 'mature' Marx (i.e. post 1845–6) are thus taken to be determinative of what Marx 'actually meant', itself a highly contentious issue and one in itself resting on rather dubious claims as to the homogeneity, consistency and thoroughness of Marx's later writings.

So what is Marxist about so-called Marxist anthropology? The first, surely, is its claim to utilise what is actually the main issue that it still needs to clarify: historical materialism. This is certainly the theme of Emmannel Terray's *Le Marxisme devant les sociétés 'primitives'* (Paris: Maspero, 1969) in which, through his analysis of the work of Lewis H. Morgan and Claude Meillassoux, he attempts not so much to *define* such an approach, but to reveal its possibility and the possibility of operationalising it in concrete social analysis, by an explication and exegesis of the texts of his chosen authors – one a pre- and indeed 'unconscious' Marxist and the other Terray's contemporary. The problem that emerges from Terray's own text itself is threefold: (i) how to define an historical materialist approach; (ii) how to develop from it or within it concepts which can be successfully used in empirical analysis, and (iii) how to define the objects and units of study to which this science of historical materialism can be applied, especially as Terray essentially wishes to retain the subject matter of traditional anthropology, although he circuitously replaces the term 'primitive' with the phrase 'socioeconomic formations in which the capitalist mode of production is absent and in which ethnologists and historians collaborate' (Terray, ibid., English edition (London: Monthly Review Press, 1972) p. 184). These questions again, having been successfully posed by Terray, are still open ones, as he himself very frankly admits.

Terray's *method* – and in particular his re-reading of texts, shows up very clearly the great influence that Althusser has had on the emergence of a 'Marxist' anthropology, and this is true in terms of his method, his claims as to the status of the later as opposed to the younger Marx, his literary style and his concentration on the concept of mode of production. The confusion that this latter issue has engendered stems in part from the claims made in the introduction to Terray's volume that 'the fundamental concepts of historical materialism are themselves being transformed in such a way as to produce exact studies in a new and specific field' (p. 2). This remarkable claim refers us back to an earlier point: how exactly the *fundamental* concepts of historical materialism can be altered and one still claim that one is operating within *Marxism* is a mystery as yet unclarified. The results of this process, however, are clearly seen in the debate about modes of production set off by Althusser. The problem here is that there is absolutely no consensus amongst Marxist anthropologists as to (i) whether modes of production actually exist at all; (ii) if they do, about how to define them; (iii) if there are, how they relate to one another, co-exist, change, disappear, articulate, etc.; and (iv) again, assuming that indeed there *are* modes of production (Marx after all was certain that there were!), how many of them there are. The extraordinary proliferation of modes of production (domestic, lineage, African, Colonial ...)suggests that in a mode of analysis that prides itself on its rigour, something has gone seriously wrong. Essentially there seems to be only one real answer to this: to return to Marx's own texts and to define on the basis of careful exegesis of these, what is meant by a mode of production. Only it would seem on the basis of such a definition are the other questions soluble, approachable and even askable *The clarification of the concept of the mode of production is the first prerequisite in operationalising (and thus ultimately validating) the analytical apparatus of historical materialism.*

Only once these preliminaries have been achieved (together with clarification of related terms such as that of 'social formation') can Marxist anthropology realistically move on to the concrete analysis of real problems. But assuming that this can be done, the problems which have emerged as the central ones, and which require further imaginative work, can be defined and perhaps clarified a little.

Given the desire (certainly as expressed in practice and professional affiliation if not in theory) of Marxist anthropologists to remain within the general problematic of pre- and non-Marxist anthropology (the continuing emphasis on Africa, on 'simple' societies, etc.), there has been an obvious continuity of interest with conventional social anthropology. There are undoubtedly both intellectual and sociological reasons for this – the continuing power of the conventional paradigm(s), their near monopoly on acedemic positions, etc, but whatever the exact background to this it has resulted in the single most conspicuous concrete advance of Marxist anthropology (and especially its French varieties): the attempt to apply historical materialism to segmentary, lineage-based societies. This in turn has resulted in a whole group of subsiduary innovations – including the critique of the 'distributionist' theory of economic anthropology, analysis of relations of production (including work units, forms of co-operation, etc), the organisation of productive activities and their technical basis, analysis of concepts of resources and commodities, the study of the sexual division of labour and of age as a principle of stratification. Ultimately these all tend to point to two 'Macroissues' – that of the status of kinship in Marxist analysis and that of the existence of classes in stateless societies. As each of these in turn generates a whole set of issues we will deal with them at some greater length.

As is well known, the problem of the analysis of kinship has dominated British social anthropology, at least since the 1940s. It is often argued within this tradition that kinship is the basis of all other social institutions (at least within the sphere of 'primitive' societies). This is obviously at variance with the fundamental premise of Marxism that the economy is the determining factor. Yet even the most Marxist of anthropologists could hardly deny the extraordinary significance of kinship in simpler societies. The problem has been then how to relate these two: economy and kinship. This is not simply an empirical question (as it is usually conceived within British social anthropology, e.g. of bridewealth or dowry as examples of links between the two). Rather it raises some fundamental theoretical questions which Marxist anthropology must confront if it is to establish its own autonomy and viability. These questions may be summarised as follows: (i) the relationship of base and superstructure, when, as in the case of 'primitive' societies, the base *is* (or appears to be) the superstructure: i.e. when kinship is the determinant, not the economy; (ii) the expansion, clarification and empirical analysis of the concept and activity of 'reproduction'; (iii) clarification of the role of the elders in relationship to the juniors, and of men in relation to women, in 'kinship' societies; (iv) the analysis of kinship as an ideology, and indeed in some cases as a mystification.

This set of questions immediately gives rise to two other very closely related ones: (i) do relationships of inequality (as found between the sexes and between elders and juniors in stratified societies) necessarily indicate a *relationship* of exploitation? and (ii) does this stratification constitute *class*? Taken together these three issues: the status of kinship, the existence and nature of exploitation and the existence of classes form a mutually interlinked and supporting triangle. And in the definition of their content and relationship, to a great extent the project of Marxist anthropology stands or falls. This is especially true when it is remembered that these elements, individually and together, must, if the project is to remain either coherent or Marxist, be analysed by the methods of historical materialism: it must be totalising, it must succeed in demonstrating the fundamental status of the economic in the whole equation. And yet at the same time nearly any anthropologist would also claim that it cannot be mechanical (it must take account of the actual complexity of relationships) and it must be true to the ethnographic richness of the concrete data. All too often one reads Marxist analyses which are sterile precisely because they are abstract, when Marx's own project was concrete. Anthropology is after all in the last analysis about people: the co-ordination of rigorous analysis and rich data is still something that offers itself as a very real challenge to Marxist anthropology.

Central then as this group of questions is, it certainly does not exhaust the list of issues still to be exhaustively tackled by Marxist anthropology. Of these, two stand out as especially significant – the questions of *Ideology* and of *Power*. The first of these, of course, stems directly from Marx himself and is largely responsible for the development of what has come to be known as the sociology of knowledge. Its role in anthropology, however, is as yet unclear. In conventional social anthropology the question has usually been swept under the carpet of 'belief systems' which is taken to include all forms of mental culture and their manifestations. But this approach, on the one hand, fails to discriminate accurately between the varieties of belief (religion, mythology, superstition, political theories etc.) and, on the other, fails to develop a systematic theory of the relationship of varieties of belief to one another and of all of them to their social basis and history. The theory of ideology is not then a peripheral topic to do with the secondary analysis of the 'superstructure' (the real effort being put into analysis of the material base.) In fact it is absolutely central to the analysis of any social formation and is precisely the field in which such topics apparently as diverse as kinship, religion and the economy are integrated. Some important steps have been taken in this direction in the works of Marc Augé, but much still remains to be done. One might argue indeed that this should be the major growth point and focus of immediate attention in Marxist anthropology. The initial step should certainly be an attempt to define and map out an anthropological theory of ideology from a Marxist perspective.

But additionally the question of ideology poses another question which has just begun to emerge on the horizon of Marxist anthropology – that of *power*. The discussion of ideology (and with it such issues as that of class) must inevitably raise the question of power, not simply as defined in conventional political terms, but as a pervasive factor in social life. The question of ideology must lead to the question of power: not only must it do so logically, but as an intellectual and political priority of Marxist anthropology it should be encouraged to emerge, not because an adequate theory of power yet exists, but precisely because it does not. This in turn provides a basis for further transforming traditional ideas within the conventional anthropological problematic about politics, kinship, economy, religion and socialisation and indeed even the central concept of culture itself.

The elaboration of a theory of ideology feeds back also to two other issues. The first of these is that of the definition of the unit of anthropological analysis as a 'social formation' and the links of this with the aforementioned problems of the mode of production concept. The second is slightly different, as it relates to the concept of *totality*. This is an idea not well elaborated in classical Marxism, but nevertheless is implicit there in Marx's method and philosophical and anthropological presuppositions. It has, furthermore, affinities with the conventional anthropological idea of holism. The idea of totality implies a number of things of great significance to anthropologists: the unit of analysis as an integrated whole not split arbitrarily into disciplinary or institutional subdivisions (the economy, the political system, etc.); the unity of theory and practice as expressed in method; the possibility of studying concrete people in the concrete socio-historical nexus in which they find themselves, without more arbitrary divisions into subjective and objective, emic and etic, and so on. As an *idea* totality is powerfully attractive, but the question for the Marxist anthropologist quite simply is: how can one operationalise it?

We need here perhaps to draw a distinction between those ideas, found in Marx himself and those inspired by him, but not directly found in the canon of his works. Each of these categories needs a brief mention here. In the first we would place a list of problems and questions which we would address to Marxist anthropology, but which have not yet occupied any major role there (due no doubt in part at least to the preoccupation with segmentary societies and with the modes of production debate). These issues would include the following: the appropriation of nature (a question so far only addressed seriously by Godelier); the concept of alienation and its relevance in the context of pre-capitalist societies, questions of objectification, reification, fetishism, tax, rent, proletarianisation; the theories of labour, of surplus value and their relationship to anthropological concepts of work; the role and status of the components of the 'superstructure' and elucidation of the concept of mediation between base and superstructure in concrete terms, the re-analysis (already in progress in some cases) of classical Marxist ideas of the Asiatic Mode of Production, of primitive communism, of the slave mode of production; and close attention to the whole debate on the applicability of Marxist ideas to non-western societies.

The second category is rather different, and relates to those ideas implied or inspired by Marx, but which he did not elaborate himself. There would include clarification of the debates on anthropology in relationship to colonialism and imperialism (which is a subject by no means yet exhausted); the development of a critique of positivistic sociologies and anthropologies; the recognition of the role of history (critical for Marx himself in the social sciences which of course did not exist at his time of writing in their present form); the elaboration of the dialectical method in anthropology; the building of useful analytical tools such as that of the concept of petty commodity production; and the building of better bridges between Marxist anthropology and the sociology of knowledge, and in particular developments in what has come to be known as (following the 'Frankfurt School') critical sociology. Marxist anthropologists, despite theoretical protestations to the contrary, have not yet broken fully out of self-imposed disciplinary isolation. There are no doubt other topics that could be pursued here, but I would like to single out four for special mention: the problem of underdevelopment; the problem of women (and children); the problem of conflict and the problem of the peasantry.

The whole issue of underdevelopment is a recent, indeed post-war, one. Yet in the last two decades it has mushroomed into an enormous industry. Marx did not talk about development as such. What he did talk about were imperialism, colonialism, the expansion of capitalism, alienation and what he believed to be the nature of non-European societies. Bourgeois sociology has appropriated to itself many of these issues and institutionalised them under the rubric 'the sociology of development'. Yet the ideas of the currently existing sociology of development would have been scarcely possible at all (especially its critical varieties) were it not for the ideas of Marx, as mediated by others such as A. G. Frank. In such hands, the basic inspiration of Marx has been in the process of being transformed into a set of powerful analytical tools for the understanding of colonial, post-colonial and peripheral capitalist societies, the links between underdevelopment and the expansion of metropolitan capitalism, and the crucial link between the system of colonialism and the very existence of underdevelopment. Marx himself, of course, did not see things in quite this way. Indeed he is notorious for having represented colonialism (for example in India) as an objectively progressive force which broke down the Asiatic communalism and laid the infrastructural basis for the emergence of the capitalism from which the proletarian revolution would eventually spring. But *implicit* in his work (and especially in his views on the expansion of capitalism and alienation) is quite another point of view – and one which has proved immensely fruitful in the subsequent conceptualisation of underdevelopment. The linking up of Marxist anthropology and the study of underdevelopment has, of course, begun (Rey, Kahn, Seddon, Clammer) and much of the work of the other Marxist anthropologists suggests the beginnings of a systematic model for exploring this relationship. But in detail this still remains to be done, and suggests itself as a practical priority given the necessity of forging political links between anthropology and the world of pressing problems and change outside the academy.

The second issue is that of women (and by extension other frequently underprivileged groups such as children and the elderly). Marx himself saw the issue of women not as an item in itself on his own agenda, but as an aspect of his wider analysis of capitalism. To some extent Engels rescued it from this peripheral position in his *Origin of the Family, Private Property and the State*, but it has never achieved any central status within 'classical' Marxism, although again, as with underdevelopment, the general radicalisation stemming from many of Marx's ideas have found their way

into the contemporary women's movement. But I would suggest
that the centrality of the issue of women lies right at the centre of the
project of Marxist anthropology precisely because of the pivotal
role ascribed to the concept of *reproduction*. Yet in many of the
analyses of the French Marxist anthropologists women only
appear (along with 'cadets', juniors, etc.) as some sort of abstract
principle which is mechanically necessary for reproduction, both
biologically and of the social unit, to take place. Only the
beginnings of a critique of these positions have so far begun to
emerge ('Engendered Structures: Some Problems in the Analysis
of Reproduction', Olivia Harris and Kate Young, in Kahn and
Llobera, *The Anthropology of Pre-Capitalist Societies*). But clearly this
issue has not only political and ideological significance, but also a
crucial theoretical significance for the elaboration of any account,
itself central to the Marxist anthropological problematic, of
reproduction. And indeed we might extend this to comment that
the vague and nebulous role ascribed to most such social units
(women, children, caste groups, etc.) in the Marxist scheme needs
immediate rectification. And since the study of such groups already
lies within or close to anthropology, that would seem the sensible
place to do so. Certainly within Marxist anthropology this question
cannot be avoided much longer if credibility is to be fully achieved.

The third category of issues is that of *conflict*. Structural-functionalist anthropology, including the whole French tradition
stemming from Durkheim and the British tradition stemming
especially from Radcliffe-Brown, has stressed integration. But
Marx, of course, did not. However, except for some still embryonic
discussion of struggles between 'elders' and 'cadets', this theme has
not appeared to any great extent in Marxist anthropology. We
could divide our questions into several categories as follows: the
functions (and necessity?) of conflict, even in the simplest societies;
war in its relationship to other social processes (slavery, territorial
expansion etc.); concepts of revolution in pre-capitalist societies
and the elucidation of the concept of *social transformation* (succession
of modes of production, etc.), a question that will once again bring
Marxism into a dialogue with structuralism (as has already
occurred) in the works of Godelier.) Put briefly the issue is this: that
Marxist anthropology has not yet fully assimilated either Marx's
thinking on social evolution or elaborated for itself (or entered into
dialogue with conventional anthropology on) a theory of social
change.

Finally, there is the issue of the peasantry. It is well known that Marx's own views on the historical and sociological significance of the peasantry were negative. But while this problem has given rise to sterile Marxicological debates about the 'legitimacy' of the Chinese, Vietnamese and other agrarian revolutions, it has not in practice prevented the rapid development of an important new sub-field of development studies and rural sociology – notably peasant studies. Hence this again is by way of inspiration rather than direct influence. Since a growing body of work of Marxist and neo-Marxist anthropologists is being directed to the peasantry, attention needs to be devoted especially to two basic tasks: the definition of the peasantry from a Marxist viewpoint and the clarification of the status of the peasantry within Marxist historiography and sociology.

To draw this discussion to a close, we should also reflect on the implications of the relationships of a revitalised Marxist anthropology with conventional socio-cultural anthropology. It seems inevitable that some such dialogue must take place and it would clearly be better to begin on a positive approach. This suggests a number of ideas, the first being that conventional social anthropology, despite its stress on holism, is not itself by any means a unified problematic. On the contrary, it contains numerous different and often contradictory paradigms. Marxist anthropology can suggest a fruitful line of approach to the resolution of these contradictions and the eliminations of paradigms which are not viable as serious approaches to society. But this means that Marxism will have to confront a number of positions, such as phenomenology, about which it has hitherto had little or nothing to say. This should provide a deeply enriching experience for the Marxist tradition, if approached with imagination and an open mind and not in a sectarian spirit. Similarly conventional anthropology is actually a multi-disciplinary activity which includes not only the more obvious topics (politics, kinship, economics), but also subjects such as symbolism, mythology and linguistics. Again it is currently the case that Marxism has very little to say about these, yet there is no doubt at all that they are significant and legitimate domains. In addition to a direct confrontation with these domains, this suggests a number of other approaches, which may be listed briefly as follows: (i) dialogue on the basis of social anthropology's concept of *holism* and the Marxist concept of *totality*: are they the same? What are the differences? etc.; (ii) elaboration of the unity of theory and practice (*praxis*) as applies to field work methods; (iii) the detailed investigation of a unified approach to society and history (a debate already begun in, for example, the exchange between J. P. Sartre and C. Lévi-Strauss); (iv) a debate with social anthropology on the basis of these domains that *do* overlap, such as markets and exchange (the 'production versus distribution' issue), the nature of lineage societies, are *pre-* or *non-*capitalist and if the former the processes of their incorporation into the cash economy, demographic processes and their relationship to social structure (a question that has been opened up by Godelier, for instance), and indeed the wider questions of the conceptualisation of specific varieties of 'social formations', the autonomy of kinship, religion, etc. and the universal validity of such shared concepts as determination, dominance, dependency, and dialectic.

To some extent this debate has already begun – it has issued, for example, in the 'political economy' concept being once again revived and applied in numerous situations. It shows itself in the debate about 'rationality', as defined by Godelier, on the one hand, and those who have followed Evans-Pritchard's formulation of the problem, on the other. And it shows itself to the extent that many obscurities in Marxist anthropology have been highlighted by a more conventional critique, including the Africocentrism of much of the French writing, and the extent to which it is still neo-colonial, still metropolitan Europeans studying the Third World.

But above all, this revitalisation of Marxist anthropology is really now at a cross-roads where it's fulfilment as a totalising, historical science of all human societies rests on three issues: (i) its ability to define itself, to purge itself of the economistic, deterministic vestiges of vulgar Marxism and a crude, simple-minded materialism, and to rediscover its source texts not on the basis of Marxicological exegesis (an approach which Marx himself would firmly have rejected), but of inspiration; (ii) its ability to return to and reflect certain basic premises of Marxism which have somehow got lost – such as the central concern with social *justice*; and (iii) its preparedness to break out of its conventional economic mould and to confront issues of belief, language, art, and so on. What Marxist anthropology does not yet have, but which it needs most urgently, is a *theory of culture*, part of which will surely be an anthropological grappling with the central

Marxist concept of *alienation*. And what can be the outcome of this? Essentially a new anthropology, one which is critical and reflexive, one which transcends the boundaries of conventional anthropology, one which unites theory and practice and one which concretises in itself and in its analyses the principle of *totality*. One parting shot: we have had far too much of Althusser. One of the forgotten themes in all anthropology today is that of *philosophical anthropology*, which starts from the question 'What is Man?' Marx himself tried to answer this question – the *early* Marx that is, and it is from exactly this source that a new anthropology, divorced from crude economism, emancipated fully from its colonial heritage, no longer confined to the 'simple' societies but to the complex as well, can emerge: a genuine *science* of *Man*. Whether or not one is a Marxist this must be seen as the only viable starting point for a new anthropology: precisely because it is only in confrontation with Marxism that the critical questions emerge with startling clarity.

6   Engels's Anthropology Revisited

The work of Frederick Engels, and in particular his *The Origin of The Family, Private Property and the State*, forms a kind of watershed in the history of anthropological thinking about matrifocal kinship. *The Origin of the Family* is pivotal in that it is the work which summarises, synthesises and transmits the earlier tradition of Morgan, Bachofen *et al.*, while simultaneously formulating a materialist interpretation of kinship which has resurfaced within anthropology with such writers as Meillassoux, and outside anthropology with the Marxist sector of the women's liberation movement. It is the nature and significance of this pivotal position that I wish to examine. I will do this by briefly summarising Engels's substantive theory, by assessing what has and what has not been established by this theory, by examining some of Engels's commentators in the light of this, and by considering the implications for anthropological studies of kinship of the questions posed by Engels. For it is at least an arguable contention that Engels is not primarily significant for the accuracy of what he wrote so much as for the problems which he posed.

Engels himself regarded his work as derivative in two senses – in that he was simply fulfilling a bequest and presenting material that Marx had been unable to complete because of his death, and also that the object of the book is to represent Morgan's findings in the light of Marx and Engels's own conclusions, and to re-establish Morgan as a discoverer of the materialist conception of history. The analytical objective of the exercise, therefore, is to establish the history of the family in the light of this particular theory of history, of which Engels says,

> According to the materialist conception, the determining factor in history is, in the last resort, the production and reproduction

of immediate life. But this itself is of a twofold character. On the one hand, the production of the means of subsistence, of food, clothing and shelter and the tolls requisite therefore; on the other the production of human beings themselves, the propagation of the species.[1]

Engels thus begins his work, appropriately enough, with a history of the human family, based on Morgan's categorisation of the stages of culture, noteably, (i) Savagery, (ii) Barbarism, and (iii) Civilisation.[2] This in turn provides a model of the evolution of the human family, which itself falls into seven stages. The first of these is the original condition of promiscuous intercourse. The second is the *Consanguine Family* in which it is alleged that marriage groups are formed in which incest of an intra-generational type is normal. This form of family, according to Engels's, no longer exists but represents a 'necessary preliminary stage' in the evolutionary scheme. The third form is the *Punaluan Family* in which both parents and children and brothers and sisters are excluded from mutual sexual intercourse. This system represents the origin of the *gens* or clan, since in Lévi-Strauss' terminology it marks the point of transition from nature to culture, or in other words the moment at which *kinship* becomes possible. Organisationally the Punaluan family is characterised by its communistic common households. As Engels put it,

> This is the classical form of the family structure which later admitted of a series of variations, and the essential characteristic feature of which was mutual community of husbands and wives within a definite family circle, from which, however, the brothers of the wives – first the natural brothers, and later the collateral brothers also – were excluded, the same applying conversely to the sisters of the husbands.[3]

This is an example in other words, of *group marriage*, and is also alleged to illustrate the origins of mother right or matriarchy, since individual fathers cannot be known.

The fourth stage of the family is represented by Engels as being the *Pairing Family*, in which habitual pairing between individuals leads to the establishment of loose marriage ties. Gradually an increasing range of marriage prohibitions between relatives comes to be established (and indeed only now can relatives as a concept be defined). Such a system remains communistic, households still exist and women continue to enjoy high status partly because the paternity problem still remains.

The fifth stage of the family is seen as the state of transition from matriliny to patriliny, as a result of concentration of wealth in the hands of the males, with the associated demand that inheritance be reckoned through the male line. The actual date of this cultural revolution remains buried in prehistory, but 'That it was actually *affected* is more than easily proved by the abundant traces of motherright which have been collected ... How easily it is accomplished can be seen from a whole number of Indian tribes, among whom it has only recently taken place and is still proceeding.'[4] This in turn is succeeded by the sixth stage, that of the transition from *patriliny* to *patriarchy*, and finally by the transition from patriarchy to monogamy via polygamy. The achievement of monogamy represents a paradox for it is not only 'one of the signs of the beginning of civilization', but it also represents a microcosm of capitalist society, in that it contains the first major antagonism or contradiction of civilised society, that between the man and the repressed female.[5]

How are we to assess the validity of this theory and it's socio-political overtones? The answer to this falls into three parts: (i) the empirical accuracy of Engels's and Morgan's anthropological beliefs, (ii) the views and commentaries of their contemporary supporters, who number not a few, and (iii) the problem of ideology in kinship studies, of which there are two subsections, (a) the problem of the patriarchial interpretation of matrilineal kinship, and (b) the problem of Idealism *v.* Materialism in the study of kinship.

The first general problem is that of the anthropological status of the Engels/Morgan 'scheme' and particularly how it stands as a 'model' of history rather than as an empirical account. Thus as Terray puts it, 'In a word, it was not Morgan's purpose to describe the different stages of human social evolution, or to write a history of humanity, but to construct a *theory* of that history, that is, a system of concepts to make it possible to 'think it out scientifically.'[6] In other words, it is a theory that is both materialistic and structural, and is therefore to be judged by the appropriate canons of criticism of these philosophies rather than by the misleading and inappropriate ones of positivism. The stages of the evolution of the family are thus to be regarded not as inevitable (the origin of the *gens*, for example, can be found in both the consanguine and Punaluan systems), but rather as a *logical* sequence, i.e. as general laws of cultural development and not as actual historical sequences.

Not all Engels's supporters see the situation in exactly the same light, however. The introduction to the present edition of *The Origin of the Family* is a good example of this. Engels's work is here seen as a thesis 'to arm the (feminist) movement theoretically', or as a work of inspiration rather than of facts. The work is also seen, *contra* Terray, to be evolutionist in the normally understood sense of the term. Anthropological societies are also seen as being characterised by the complete absence of private property, 'complete equality in all spheres of life', and with an elective, egalitarian political system,[7] all of which are, of course, completely mythical. This is coupled with an attack on the anti-historicist tendencies of much modern anthropology but with no understanding of why anthropology came to reject precisely the kind of conjectural history that Engels and his commentator are advocating. Yet paradoxically, while making the astounding error of lumping the diffusionists with the functionalists and structuralists, Malinowski is praised when (and because) he describes Trobriand matrilineality! This kind of argumentation in fact only serves to weaken Engels's perfectly serious attempt to arrive at some valid anthropological generalisations based on the (now long superceded) information that he had available to him *at the time*, by making his project appear simply ridiculous.

It in any case fails to come to terms with the central proposition of the thesis – that of the link between patriarchial kinship and property. Is it true, analytically speaking? Alternatively, phrased in more contemporary terminology, this raises the question of the relationship between production and procreation,[8] and of the bearing of this on the interpretation of kinship systems. Before going on to try to answer this we need to make some prefaratory theoretical remarks. These relate to the two linked considerations, what are the connections between kinship groups and the economy? and what are the connections between economic processes and the processes of reproduction? These issues are important because they call into question the British anthropological tradition of giving the primacy in anthropological analysis, both empirical and theoretical, to kinship studies, as well as the position associated with Lévi-Strauss which excludes the economic factor in favour of a concept of 'kinship autonomy' based on his general theory of communication model.

But what will happen if we invert the traditional view and begin not with the kinship system as the basic stratum of social life, but with the economy, and regard it, at least for heuristic purposes, as the basis, and then go on to explore how it operates to generate the kinship system with which it is associated? Terray has a very pertinent comment to make about this when he remarks as follows:

> In a more general way, the process of making kinship into a simple theoretical entity seems to me no better than the invention of 'totemism' so justly condemned by Lévi-Strauss: it brings together under one heading systems whose positions and functions are not the same in every socio-economic formation. Some of these systems organize social life as a whole, while others effect only some sectors, and these again differ widely; in some cases it may be production, in others consumption, or in still others marriage contracts. To give kinship studies a strategically decisive value for the under-standing of primitive societies 'kinship' must be understood as something more than a simple combination of terms and attitudes, and kinship systems must be considered in their functional aspect as much as in their formal aspect: at this point the unity of the entity 'kinship' can no longer be thought of as given and has to be proved.[9]

In Marxist terms, in other words, we are speaking of the balance between determination by the base and the autonomy of aspects of the superstructure. It is even arguable that in primitive societies kinship relations are the structural equivalent of class relations in capitalist or feudal systems. In concrete analysis the understanding of this will require the examination of the complex interplay of the economic, juridico-political and ideological aspects of the mode of production (or of Althusser's notion of 'superdetermination' or conjunction of several determinations in a single 'object').

But the profound differences between 'kinship' societies and those based on class leads us, in Terray's words, 'back to the thesis supported by Engels and Morgan in the first applications of historical materialism to ethnology: the domination of kinship relations in the social organization is incompatible with the exploitation of labour and the existence of class relations'.[10] This very interesting subject leads into many issues, for example, the question of whether exploitation can exist in 'kin' societies which cannot be touched on here, but which have been explored elsewhere.[11] The critical issue here is rather that of the nature of the internal relationship between the economy and the kinship system: 'Kinship does not play a determining role alongside the economy, since it is itself an element of the economic infrastructure.'[12] In philosophical terms this is a dispute between a materialistic and an idealistic conception of kinship, the latter which sees kinship systems essentially as logical systems or as systems or categories. (Again Lévi-Strauss is a prime example of this position.)

To return, therefore, to Engels in the light of this theoretical digression, we have to ask ourselves where the accuracies and inaccuracies of Engels's theory lie. There are two categories of problems: empirical ones and conceptional ones, which we will take in that order.

The empirical ones can be stated and summarised as follows: (i) The status of the evolutionary hypothesis as applied to human societies rather than just to animal ones; (ii) Problems of the actual historical existence of some of the kinship systems mentioned, for example group marriage which seems never to have existed in any recorded case in the form imagined by Engels; (iii) The confusion of existing primitive societies with *prehistoric* ones from the remote past. To Engels they have equal status in that the former are seen as being just contemporary examples of the latter; (iv) Failure to discriminate geographically: do some systems only evolve in certain circumstances, ecological or otherwise, or do they all evolve through the same sequence everywhere and invariably, and if the latter, what is the hidden mechanism of this evolution? This is in fact a thorny question for if the sequence of evolution is the same everywhere then materialism has to explain, in non-idealist terms, why it is that differing ecologies do *not* produce corresponding variations in structural type; (v) Problems of the explanation of the evolution of matrifocal systems into systems of a different type. This involves a number of clarifications, one being the distinction, not acknowledged by Engels, between *matriarchial* and *matrilineal*; another being the problem of the evolution of cognatic systems and of other complex systems such as polygyny, where the man marries wives who are not sisters. A very interesting case is also brought to light by the work of Jaspan, who examines an example from Sumatra where the evolutionary direction in the kinship system of the Redjang people appears to be in the opposite direction from that expected by Engels – in this case from patriliny to matriliny.[13] Jaspan's example also casts some doubt on the evolutionary belief that each form of descent is mutually exclusive. In this context Engels gives no weight at all, for example, to the importance of relations with matri- or patri-kin *regardless* of the structural type of the kinship system.

The second group of problems are the conceptual ones. This again requires us to look at the theoretical background to the problem. Fox distinguishes three main varieties of matrilineal organisation. The first is that based on the mother–brother–sister roles and matrilocal residence. Here the burden of control and continuity is to some extent shifted on to the women, and in societies with this basis it is usually the case that women have higher prestige and influence than in the others. The second is that based on the brother–sister–nephew roles, with avunculocal residence preferred, or, failing this, some means whereby the mother's brother can control his nephews. In this type, the status of women is usually lower as control and continuity are primarily in the hands of the men. The third is that based on the full constellation of consanguine matrilineal roles – mother daughter, brother/sister, mother's brother/sister's son. Here the control and continuity are primarily in the hands of the men, but the *status* of the women need not be low.[14] Only the first of the three types approaches genuine 'matriarchy'. So why then are there problems with matrilineal systems? Is this simply an empirical question, that we are not so used to dealing with them because they are fairly rare? The answer to this is no, as we can see if we look more closely at the problems arising. To return again to Fox who lists four main principles of kinship, notably, (i) that the women have the children, (ii) the men impregnate the women, (iii) the men exercise control, and (iv) primary kin do not mate with one another. The interesting thing about this list is that item three is qualitatively different from the others. *Why* and *how* do the men come to exercise this control and why did the women lose it if they had it in the first place?

As we have seen, part of the problem for Engels arises from the false belief that in a system with descent through the females these same females also hold and exercise the social power. In fact the difficulty in grasping the principles of matrilineal systems is that while patrilineal ones combine authority, descent and residence, they do not provide such a neat solution. *Theoretically* they could, but in practice they do not. The 'Amazonian' solution, however delightful as a romantic idea, does not seem to have existed anywhere in reality. Also as Engels did perceive, problems of paternity need not disturb matrilineal societies, yet they continue to maintain the institution of marriage, even though it is logically a marginal entity. There is also another point worth mentioning, which is that many anthropologists persist in seeing patrilineal systems as the paradigm of kinship organisation, and therefore, consciously or not, regard the other structural types as deviant cases. The asymmetry between them is explained by the different relationships that they have to descent, authority and residence as noted above, so matrilineal ones, yet there is a tendency for anthropologists to treat them as if they were. They are not mirror images precisely because of the role, status and power distinction between the men and the women. There is in any case another important structural distinction between patrilineal and matrilineal systems, notably that in the former the *wives* are the significant female members, while in the latter it is the *sisters* of the men who are significant in terms of the continuity and reproduction of the lineage. This has important consequences for the role of women in the two systems, in terms of roles, recruitment, status and power over the disposition of property, both within their own lineage (from which they came) and the lineage of the husband, this distinction is also another reason why the two systems are not mirror images of one another. It is also for this reason that the role of the husbands is so ambiguous in matrilineal societies. Incidentally, it is also worth mentioning in passing that Engels's theory, if correct, would do some damage (paradoxically since their theories derive a great deal of their inspiration from him) to the fashionable hypotheses of the French economic anthropologists such as Meillassoux, Dupré and Rey, since their view of power relations in tribal societies presupposes the existence of an unambiguously patrilineal system.[15]

The question then is, did 'matriarchy' ever exist, and if it did, was it a single indivisible entity? We have already noted the elementary distinction between matriarchy and matriliny. We know what the latter is, but what is the former? This attempt at definition does indeed raise the interesting issue, which has not received much attention from anthropologists since the subject became unfashionable, of whether the existence of 'matrilineal' institutions such as the avunculate imply that these are the vestiges of an early and more thorough-going 'motherright' society? There are a number of problems internal to this prospect, such as establishing the distinction between *descent* through the mother and *affinity* through the mother, on the one hand, and the suggestion, on the other, of a relationship between the mode of descent and the family type, such that the matriarchial complex could not include the husband/father and therefore could not include a discernible nuclear family group. Also confused, or overlooked in Engels's account, are the problems of residence (that matrilocal residence does not necessarily imply matrilineal descent) and the distinction between social and biological paternity. Engels is not at all clear about the conceptual distinctions and relationships between the notions of kinship, descent, residence, recruitment and paternity. It is also clear that the links between the sociological features of matrifocal kinship systems and their technico-economic-ecological base is not a simple one at all, but also involves the mediation of political structures as well as simple subsistence factors.[16]

If we do not then seem to have discovered matriarchy as an entity from Engels is there something else that we can learn from him? The answer is without doubt yes, and the key lies in our earlier discussion of the role of materialism in the interpretation of kinship. The importance of this approach can be seen when we contrast it with the more conventional approach. For example, Gough and Schneider, in introducing their monumental work on matrilineal kinship, define the distinctive characteristics of these systems as being, 'First, women are responsible for the care of children, with every child being the primary responsibility of one woman; second, adult men have authority over women and children; and third, descent group exogamy is required.'[17] These characteristics are all logical or idealist ones, and say nothing at all about the equally important (conceptually and empirically) economic factors, which also say a lot about how these logical factors arise.

To some extent this same criticism can be applied to Engels himself, for he saw the instability of matrifocal systems as arising solely from their inability to prevent male dominance from encroaching as a result of changing property relationships. There are additional structural and ideological reasons for the instability of these systems. Amongst these factors are the 'ambiguous' status of the men; on the potential strain which arises from the fact that the sister is a tabooed sexual object to her brother, yet her sexual and reproductive activities remain a matter of permanent interest to him; on the fact that matrilineal systems do not require the statuses of father and husband, which can thus vary within very wide limits, while at the same time the ideology of descent which ignores or minimises the male role in conception puts the in-marrying male in a position where despite his biological contribution he can be socially minimised, which naturally offends his political sensibilities. Another group of problems can be listed including the facts that the institutionalisation of strong ties between husband and wife is not compatible with the maintenance of matrilineal descent groups, so limits must be set to the authority of husbands, which is presumably part of the explanation for the association so often found between the avunculate and matrilineal systems; problems of bridewealth; the fact that bonds between a child and its father are likely to be in competition with the authority stemming from the mother's descent group; the fact that while women bring a sense of loyalty to the patrilineage that they join, men do not bring a corresponding loyalty to their matrilineage and finally that small or isolated matrilineal groups are very difficult to maintain. The instability of matrifocal systems is thus the result of a complex group of factors of which the relationship of the men to the property is only a part.

It helps to understand these elements better if one considers the empirical evidence of the effects of social and cultural changes on matrilineal systems. As Gough and Schneider observe:

> Recent literature has accumulated to show that under economic changes brought about with Western industrial nations, matrilineal descent groups gradually disintegrate. In their place the elementary family eventually emerges as the key kinship group with respect to residence, economic cooperation,

legal responsibility and socialization with a narrow range of interpersonal kinship relations spreading outwards from it bilaterally and linking it with other elementary families.

The cycle of evolution of matrilineal systems thus results from an interplay between the structural features of the system and the economic forces to which they are subject. Change varies considerably from one system to another in its details, but this general model appears to be valid, nevertheless.

A brief examination of some of the best known and documented examples of matrilineal systems reveals this very clearly. Amongst the Tonga the key to change appears to be the introduction of modern cash crop farming which has resulted in the accumulation of wealth well above traditional subsistence needs, which in turn increases tensions in conjugal and paternal relationships. As the mode of production changes and wealth increases the matrilineal group tends to break down, especially for purposes of inheritance, and begins to move towards an elementary family structure by way of an intermediate form of grouping composed of uterine siblings and their immediate descendants through the female line. Similarly amongst the Ndembu, the change from subsistence agriculture to cash cropping has resulted in the emergence of a basic form of the elementary family and a situation where wages are devoted to the elementary family and not to the matrilineage. Other changes can be seen as a fairly direct result of colonialism, as in Bemba or Ashanti where labour migration and cash cropping, respectively, are products of the imperial system, or yet again in Kerala where private land ownership, wage labour on the plantations and the attractions of work in government service are spin-offs of colonialism. Other cases are more complex, as with the Minangkabau where instability of the matrilineal system has manifested itself in features such as the sale of lineage-owned property, increase in private property, geographical scattering of lineages, and the emergence of extended and elementary family organisation. The role of the technico-economic base can also be seen in those systems where change has been minimal, which proves the general validity of the theory that we are suggesting. Just such an example is that of Truk where the system is relatively unchanged because copra production can still be organised on the basis of the lineage organisation, although other forms of industry such as that introduced by the Japanese cannot.

So while the evidence does indeed point to the importance of the economic factor in the explanation of change in matrilineal systems, it also contradicts Engels on another vital point, notably that the trend is for matrilineal systems to evolve not into patrilineal ones, but towards cognatic ones and/or towards extended or elementary family structures. It is also true that the forces acting on matrilineal systems are also common to patrilineal ones as well, but what is significant is their differential response. There is one further important point which can also be levelled against Engels, which is that he regarded matrifocal kinship systems as representing a particular level of social organisation, when in fact it is a type of membership which is in no way related to the cultural level. Finally it is well worth quoting Gough and Schneider's conclusion which, as they seem to realise, points the way out of the idealist cul-de-sac:

> Much work must be done before we understand where to lay the weight of emphasis in explaining the origins, maintenance and disappearance of matrilineal systems: in what connections to stress the organization of labour, the forms of property, the types of subsistence base, the contributions of the two sexes (almost certainly viewed in the context of work organization and not by itself), the level of political complexity, the nature of the authority system, the size and proximity of communities in their relationship to the technical and environmental base, and the relationship of the culture in question to other cultures. Unless some of these variables can be rejected out of hand, large scale work will be required for a final solution.[18]

These are, of course, precisely the general kind of solution that Engels is suggesting all along.

So, if we 'revisit' the anthropology of Engels in perhaps the same kind of way that Terray has revisited the work of Morgan, what do we find there and does it still justify our attention? The general outlines of a critique are contained in the account given above and do not therefore need to be repeated. What we must look at in conclusion are the more general aspects of the theory. These we may briefly summarise as follows: (i) The transmission of the work of Morgan, while often mentioned in the textbooks of anthropological theory, has in substance largely been ignored by the modern day profession. While Terray has already done a great deal to rescue Morgan from the obscurity into which he had fallen, it is really through Engels that the real impact of Morgan has been transmitted. There are two reasons for this: first, it was Engels who recognised that Morgan's work was, or contained the seeds of, the application of the materialist theory to the study of primitive and prehistoric societies, and rescued it from the oblivion into which it would otherwise have fallen by showing up its general and abiding relevance. Secondly, it is to Engels that latter-day radicals have naturally looked rather than to Morgan, who to most people is just an out of date anthropologist. The significance of *The Origin of the Family* may be that through its medium Engels transmits Morgan instead of saying anything very new himself, which he manifestly does not do. Or put another way, one could argue that *The Origins* should simply be read as a Marxist commentary on Morgan, who was the original and independent discoverer of the theories presented in the book.

A second reason for not ignoring Engels is that he raises the problem of the application of historical materialism to non-industrialised societies – even though he does not give a satisfactory answer. In this respect he is not only theoretically important in his own right, but is also the source and inspiration for the researches now being carried out by Meillassoux and his colleagues cited elsewhere in the references to this paper, and which are also discussed elsewhere in greater detail than can be attempted here.

As with any work, the book suffers from the intellectual constraints of its own era. This can be seen in its backward-looking utopianism, its reliance on purely literary and/or secondary sources, its inability to conceive of a materialist conception of kinship without the necessity of incorporating a theory of cultural stages – which is in fact quite independent of, and unnecessary to, such a conception, although it is a legitimate subject of study in its own right – and its lack of success in rigorously explaining the transition between and the inevitability (or otherwise) of these cultural stages when they are invoked. There is a final danger that the apologia for such a theory, on the basis that it is not at all empirical but conceptual (a 'model'), rapidly degenerates into fantasy unless it is given a stricter rationale and conceptual underpinning than that provided by Engels himself.

There is thus no 'balance-sheet' to be drawn up here as to whether or not it is worth continuing to pay attention to Engels in the present day. His work is fertile more in what it suggests than in what it actually establishes in its own right, and this is itself an achievement. At the very least this debate has taken us beyond a purely idealist conception of kinship and into a realm where the different aspects of social formations (economic, cultural, etc.), so often kept apart for analytical reasons, need to be occasionally reintegrated. With this kind of perspective in mind Engels can be regularly revisited with some profit, both in terms of fruitful ideas and pitfalls to avoid, by Marxists and non-Marxists alike.

NOTES AND REFERENCES

1. F. Engels, *The Origin of the Family, Private Property and the State.* Preface to the first edition, 1884. Cited from the Pathfinder Press edition, New York, 1972, p. 25. All further references are to this edition.
2. Ibid., pp. 33–4.
3. Ibid., p. 53.
4. Ibid., p. 67.
5. Ibid., pp. 71–2 and p. 75.
6. E. Terray, *Marxism and 'Primitive' Societies* (London and New York, 1972). French edition, *Le Marxisme devant les Sociétés Primitives: Deux Études* (Paris, 1969).
7. E. Reed. Introduction to *The Origin of the Family*, p. 9.
8. C.f. C. Meillassoux, 'From Reproduction to Production', *Economy and Society*, vol. 1, no. 1, 1972.
9. Terray, *Marxism and 'Primitive' Societies*, pp. 140–1.
10. Ibid., p. 156.
11. See J. R. Clammer (ed.), *The New Economic Anthropology* (London, 1978).
12. M. Godelier, *Rationality and Irrationality in Economics* (London, 1972), p. 54.
13. M. A. Jaspan, 'From Patriliny to Matriliny', Ph.D. thesis (Canberra, Australian National University, 1964).
14. Robin Fox, *Kinship and Marriage* (Harmondsworth: Penguin Books, 1967), p. 112.
15. For Meillassoux see 'From Reproduction to Production', and for Georges Dupré and P. P. Rey see their 'Reflections on the Pertinence of a Theory of the History of Exchange', in *Economy and Society*, vol. 2, no. 2, 1973.
16. Note, for example, that the Navaho and Plateau Tonga are acephalous, and loosely structured, while the Trukese and Trobrianders have settled cultivation and are organised in chiefdoms; the Ashanti have a large state organisation, Kerala is highly stratified. With residence the Plateau Tonga are irregular, the Navaho Trukese and northern Keralese are matrilocal, the Trobrianders, some Navaho and some nothern Keralese are avunculocal, while the central Keralese and Ashanti have the visiting spouse arrangement.
17. D. M. Schneider and K. Gough (eds), *Matrilineal Kinship* (Berkeley, 1961), p. 5.
18. Ibid., p. 726.

7   Power, Descent and Reproduction: A Critique of the Concept of the 'Lineage Mode of Production' in Chinese Society

One of the most lasting contributions of the recent flourishing of French neo-Marxist anthropology has been that of drawing attention to the materialist element (the 'political economy' if you like) of that most sacrosanct and frequently (in the philosophical sense) idealised province of the Anglo-Saxon social anthropology: kinship. The present chapter is an exploratory one, and therefore tentative in its conclusions, or at least in its formulation of the specific problem to which it is addressed. This may be defined as the application to the analysis of traditional Chinese society of three of the questions raised by the French neo-Marxists, namely, (i) is there such a thing as a 'lineage mode of production'? (ii) does exploitation exist in a lineage society? and (iii) do classes exist in lineage societies? Traditional Chinese society, which had the patrilineage as its focus of organisation, immediately suggests itself as a suitable subject for such an investigation. This is not only a matter of antiquarian interest – a matter of studying a society no longer in existence in mainland China – but also for the study of social dynamics. Chinese society has undergone revolutionary changes in the last thirty years, and the question arises: were some of the seeds of these changes contained in the pre-revolutionary social system?

Any lineage society, or lineage based form of social organisation, has certain key sociological characteristics – of which the most important is that it is stratified by age, generation and sex.

As a general rule those who are older (and in a case of a patrilineage the older males) exercise control over the disposal of both physical resources (land, property, tools, etc.), non-material resources (for example magic and, in the case of Chinese society, the ancestor veneration cult and its attendant rituals) and what has been termed 'social knowledge', that is, genealogies and knowledge of the rules governing marriage.[1] The pre-eminence of the elders is thus maintained by a combination of their physical age, control of property and near monopoly of essential religious and sociological knowledge. Furthermore, this control is not simply static – it extends to the control of the demographic reproduction of the lineage (who should or may marry whom, when, etc.). The successful reproduction of the conditions of production obviously follows from this: the viability of the lineage (especially if it is a physically localised one) depends upon its ability to reproduce itself, to maintain its access to resources (especially land), to be able to defend itself, to produce sufficient children of the right sex to continue the lineage, and to maintain the ancestor cult, etc. All this in turn implies a relationship of dependence between the elders and juniors (or 'cadets' as the Frenchmen have it) and between men and women, and even between the dead and the living if the ancestors are still active in their influence. The question of whether or not this relationship of dependence (which is mutual) represents one of *exploitation* is a moot point. Elsewhere I have pointed out some of the actual or potential problems with this view of lineage organisation (for example, whether goods produced by the 'cadets' are entirely controlled by the elders or whether social knowledge is really exclusive to the elders).[2] Obviously simple inequality of access to resources, or the existence of an economic surplus, does not in itself imply that there is a relationship of exploitation between those who manage the surplus and those who do not. Not only is this logically the case, but to argue that exploitation is necessarily implied is to commit oneself to a crudely materialistic view of social relations – one that ignores the non-material dimensions of power and ideology. What we must do is to address these questions to some actual ethnographic data – in this case that of traditional Chinese society.

In the pre-revolutionary Chinese countryside the main structural units of social organisation were the exogamous patrilineages, often spatially localised and frequently owning extensive landed property (especially in South China). On the whole, lineages ran their own internal affairs, including solving property disputes, policing their own members and even organising their own defence in troubled times. They were largely independent of state interference, and even those functions that were the responsibility of government – such as the collection of taxes – were often delegated to lineage elders to perform. In theory at least the lineage was free of class considerations: 'From one point of view the lineage was egalitarian: theoretically men were promoted to positions of authority according to kinship principles, and all members had equal claims on the property owned corporately by the lineage and on the ritual and secular services which it provided.'[3] But in practice it is now known that it was not the elders as such (defined genealogically) but the *gentry* elders who were the main source of power and authority. The elders were the bigger landlords, rich merchants and those who had achieved passes in the Imperial examination (i.e. the literati) and whose influence was to a great extent extra-lineage in its nature and sources. From this point of view then the lineage was most certainly *not* egalitarian and social authority, while often expressed in the idiom of kinship or reinforced by position in the kinship hierarchy, was actually extra-lineal, and was largely political, economic or educational (or all three together) in nature. Women did not feature at all in this – they did not own property, had rights only through their husbands and did not even possess their own ancestors as they were obliged to adopt those of the lineage into which they married.

The 'ideal' code of Chinese kinship thus diverges sharply from the reality (or rather realities, as there were many regional variations)[4] and the view of the lineage as a kind of cosy club in which only peace, harmony and co-operation and not a hint of competition prevail was soon questioned.[5] In fact, the evidence of intra-family feuds, lineage segmentation (usually for economic reasons) and social stratification (other than that based purely on genealogical principles) within the lineage, has become so overwhelming as to force a change of view. At least one author has tried to show this by juxtaposing the views of Freedman with those of writers from the People's Republic of China or sympathetic to it, in order to show that the 'classical' model of Chinese kinship, as now perceived from the new China, conceals contradictions and the existence of exploitation.[6] The hardships suffered by the peasants under the social organisation of the old regime have been very extensively documented, and it is of interest that the lineage organisation – especially its governance by rich clan members, its oppression of women, and its use of the supernatural as a means of social control – has been singled out for special mention again and again as evidence of the way in which it was used to serve the interests of the privileged. Accordingly it became a major focus of peasant resentment and ideological attack during, after and since the revolution, when kinship solidarity, with all its attendant parochialism and special interests, was condemned and the existence of class differences *within* kinship units was systematically pointed out for the first time.[7]

This is not to suggest that the existence of social classes was not recognised in pre-revolutionary China. The idea of major, indeed structural, inequalities in Chinese society was an early idea, and one sanctioned furthermore by the major philosophical school – Confucianism, and social status was never to be equated purely with kinship status. Confucius, and Mencius who further developed his thought, classified people not only by occupations, but into five broad categories or grades – the stupid, the learned, the superior, the worthy and the sages. Confucian ethics had enormous influence during the imperial period and indeed today still represent what some people would consider to be the essential core of Chinese culture. Hierarchy was not only considered desirable by the Confucians, but as sociologically necessary for the maintaining of order. And as the family is seen as a microcosm of the state (and vice versa), so hierarchy is also necessary in the kin relationships. This ideological underpinning had its effects in legitimising social inequalities, although it did not necessarily cause them, since the roots of actual stratification lay, as I will argue, in economics.

We have here then an interesting situation: a large scale lineage society in which recognised social classes existed on a country-wide basis. In addition to the five Confucian 'grades', four other more sociologically defined ranks were recognised – the scholars (*shih*), the farmers (*nung*), the artisans (*kung*) and the merchants (*shang*). These gradations again refer to the 'ideal type' (in Weber's sense) of the social organisation, and they were not 'castes' in the sense of being automatically hereditary and without opportunities for individuals to be socially mobile. In fact, both

individuals and whole lineages could rise and fall in the status
system, and in practice the rural landed gentry and the urban
merchants came to dominate along with the literati beureaucracy,
who were often drawn from, or otherwise in alliance with, these
other two groups.[8] In practice it was the gentry who mediated
between lineage and government and who were the dispute-sol-
vers in local situations, and also the gentry who avoided paying
taxes, and were exempt from labour conscription.[9] Kinship then,
while of major importance in pre-revolutionary China, was not
the only element or principle of social structure.

Its importance as an *ideology* of social organisation, which has
already been indicated, expressed itself in several concrete forms.
First, was the concept of *service*: the individual was significant only
as a member of the group, and as such had certain obligations and
duties, and certain rights as well. This concept of service tended to
prevail even when the divisive features of the lineage (i.e. those
contradictions, usually of wealth, which caused segmentation to
occur) were most conspicuous. In fact even the richest and most
powerful lineage would have trouble staying that way – largely
because of the inheritance rules that would divide property
between the male members – and also because of the tendency for
one segment of a lineage to secede from the poorer parent lineage,
if that segment was able to accumulate wealth for itself. A second
factor was the attachment to the idea of filial piety. In the
traditional kinship system filial piety functioned as a powerful
mechanism of social control and as a means of perpetuating male
dominance. It was reflected in rules governing relations between
parents and children and between the children themselves (elder
brothers being superior to younger brothers, and all brothers to
all sisters), in the degrees and periods of mourning for various
categories of kin, and in actual sanctions which the family or
lineage could impose on offenders – including even the death
penalty for extreme cases of unfilial conduct.

Thirdly, it was reflected in the struggles *between* lineages. Each
lineage, according to the 'model', was expected to close ranks
against the encroachment of other lineages, theoretically identical
to itself in structure. This process naturally helped both to
reinforce the society-wide significance of the lineage principle,
and to ensure internal cohesion, or at least the appearance of such
cohesion. In south China, struggles between lineages often took
the form of *feng-shui* fighting, that is, the use of geomancy to

enhance one's own good fortune and to diminish that of others by way of the auspicious sighting of graves and buildings, and the tampering with the graves of the 'opposition'. A fourth feature was the maintaining of the patriarchal principle. In traditional society a woman had very few rights in the lineage into which she married and could be divorced for numerous reasons, including 'jealousy' and neglect of her parents-in-law. The patriarchal principle provided the underpinning for the male domination of family and lineage affairs. Finally, the traditional lineage was seen by its members as being in many ways opposed to the State – or at the least to State interference in its internal affairs. Where the State was weak, the lineages would be virtually self-governing mini-states, organising their own defence and making war on one another. In such cases clans – i.e. federations of lineages – would sometimes appear to increase the political, economic or military weight of a group of people putatively related to one another by possession of a common surname.

Thus the lineages, while maintaining the outward image of cohesion and unity, actually present a rather different picture on closer examination, being divided along the lines of male/female, father/child, brother/brother, rich sibling/poor sibling, although all to some extent held together by, and paying lip service to, the 'kinship principle' as a bond transcending such economic and sexual divisions.[10]

But let us return to the more theoretical aspects of the problem. It should be quite clear that the Chinese lineage (even when it was territorially localised) was not an example of what Meillassoux calls 'sociétés traditionnelles d'auto-subsistance' (traditional self-subsistence societies), since they were part of a wider economic sphere in which market relationships, monetisation, and State interference were already well developed. His theory of segmentary, lineage-based societies is thus not directly transferable to the Chinese case.[11] Additionally we have a problem: Meillassoux regards economic organisation organised along lineage principles as a *mode of production*, for which he has been rightly criticised by Terray on the grounds that, first, the mere enumeration of a set of economic activities does not constitute a mode of production in any useful sense and, secondly, that to do so 'implies that they all have the *same* mode of production; this means abandoning any attempt to explain the great variety of social and ideological relations observed in such societies', which in turn means abandoning an attempt to apply Marxist methods to 'primitive' societies.[12] An entire society of relatively undifferentiated and structurally identical lineages in which the three components of a mode of production – economic base, juridico-political superstructure and ideological superstructure – co-exist, would form a single mode of production in which the forces, relations and techniques of production stood in a fixed (and single) relationship to one another. But such a model will not fit the Chinese case, which as we have seen was differentiated by class and occupation, contained numerous local variations (lineages were much stronger in the south than in the north, for example), and in which each lineage formed a *unit* of production within the overall mode (or rather collection of modes) of production in the country as a whole – semi-feudal peasant farming in the countryside, merchandising and petty commodity production in the towns and compradore capitalism in the southern treaty ports. The word 'unit' is used here advisedly, for as Terray expresses it: 'From the point of view of the labor force a production unit is defined by the *form of cooperation* on which it is based. In fact, as soon as a process of production requires the cooperation of several independent units of labor power, it implies a work organization, an allocation and a coordination of tasks and can, in brief, be described as a form of cooperation.'[13] The lineage, as a collection of families, is exactly such a unit.

The relations of production are those which result from the way in which the lineage exploits its economic niche – usually relatively small-scale peasant farming – using the instruments of labour – simple tools, animals and human hands, and under the control or direction of the managerial structures required to supervise the whole process – the family and ultimately the lineage heads (the 'elders'). The neat thing about lineages is that these relations of production are represented (in ideological terms) in the idiom of kinship. Forms of competition, as well as forms of co-operation and solidarity (e.g. in harvesting, or when the lineage has to 'close ranks' against strangers or an encroaching lineage) are all expressed in this idiom. There are thus extended and simple forms of co-operation, namely, masculine, feminine, child and mixed processes of work. The lineage society is a continually changing kaleidoscope of work teams (the changes being rhythmical and predictable). Thus for Meillassoux the 'production community' and the lineage are the same, and furthermore it is in the lineage that control by the elders is most marked (as opposed to in other kinds of socio-economic unit). The elders have rights by virtue of age, position in the kinship system, control over the ancestor cult and, perhaps above all, by their control over the reproduction of the lineage through their control of marriage.

In theory there is a kind of built-in democracy in this (at least for the men): as a person ages so he automatically advances up the status/control hierarchy. But in practice, as we have seen, this procedure was often, if not usually, shortcircuited by the cross-cutting influence of class: not all elders, but only those who succeeded in amassing economic or political power, would actually exercise control over the lineage. Indeed, class relationships are *able* to appear precisely because the economic base is determinant, and *not* kinship as at first seems to be the case, although the kinship idiom is retained, and may indeed influence the way in which the class relationships work (in supporting or advancing one of one's own relatives rather than a fellow class member). Matrimonial exchanges and alliances between lineages buttress these relationships, by allowing the powerful elders to manipulate less powerful individuals and thus to promote their own interests (e.g. by arranging a marriage between a member of their own and another lineage in order to cement, initiate or promote a political or economic relationship). Both those who produce and those who reproduce are thus under the direct or indirect management of the lineage elders.

It follows from this too that the lineage *itself* is not a class organisation: the lineage is not a *state* (although it sometimes tried to behave like one). Rather it is the location of the lineages in the wider society of competing lineages and non-lineage (e.g. urban) institutions (i.e. in relation to the State) which provides the opportunity for economic factors to transcend kinship ones, that allows the classes to appear. Once they have appeared, even in embryonic form, then they begin to operate within and upon the kinship (i.e. lineage) structure. And once class relationships begin to appear, the possibility of exploitation appears with them, although this is not to say that it *must* exist: in reality many smaller and poorer Chinese lineages were very undifferentiated socially, economically and in the division (including sexual division) of labour.

Three important points thus emerge from this analysis, and they can be summarised as follows: first, there is no such thing as a 'lineage mode of production'. The lineage itself forms a sociological and ideational framework within which different labour processes – farming, fishing, duck-rearing, etc. – are organised, but it is not *itself* a mode of production. It is in fact something which does not fit at all into conventional Marxist categories, although it comes closest to the idea of the 'social relations of production'. But that obviously does not exhaust the definition of the lineage, since it is not only a means of organising production – it is also a kinship system *per se* (and not therefore *reducible* to economic relations), a system of exchange, and a framework for organising and expressing religious sentiments. It is not itself merely reproduced, but is itself the mechanism of social reproduction within the context of which biological reproduction is regulated. It is not even a *combination* of modes of production, but is actually something for which no Marxist concept yet exists – a specific way of structuring economic, political and reproductive relationships and activities in such a way that they are not only ideologically, but in practice seen as being subordinated to kinship relationships. As we have seen, this can be a mystification – i.e. that politico-economic domination can be exercised through the kinship system, but it is essential to bear in mind two things: in the first place, there is no evidence that the members of the system, including those dominated, were not aware of this (the evidence from revolutionary and post-revolutionary shows this very clearly, and is partly *why* the peasantry revolted), and secondly, that the kinship 'model' was nevertheless real. Certainly it was often abused, but this did not reduce its value as an account of how things *should* be. The mode of production was thus not the lineage: the lineages themselves were rather units in what might be termed, in pre-revolutionary China and extending the European sense of the term, a feudal mode of production, and in post-revolutionary Taiwan and rural Hongkong they represent vestiges of the feudal-kinship ideology still struggling to come to terms with capitalism and to adjust to its mode of social organisation.

The second major point relates to *reproduction*. Reproduction plays a key role in understanding the lineage – indeed ideologically that is what the lineage is about. Control of reproduction (i.e. power over the regulation of marriage, residence, descent and the ancestors) is the means by which a great deal of the political domination of the elders is expressed, and is certainly the idiom in which it is normally couched, even when the actual basis of the domination is economic. An analysis of the nature of disputes (i.e. problems arising over contradictions) in Chinese lineages shows this to be very clearly the case. Control over the processes of production *allows* the elders to exercise in practice the control over reproduction already assigned to them by the kinship ideology.

Thirdly, we must conclude that *a priori* exploitation may exist in a purely technical sense in a lineage society, i.e. in a situation where the producers do not determine the disposition of surplus value, but what is of much greater interest are the situations in which exploitation, in the more commonplace use of the term, do actually occur. Similarly we must conclude that classes, in the strict sense of the term as not only economic units separated from other units as part of a stratified social whole but also as conscious of themselves as classes, do not exist within the lineage. Rather they exist in the feudal mode of production of which they are a part, and these classes are thus reflected or, in another sense of the word, 'reproduced' in the lineage. The subordination of women and the subordination of juniors (of both sexes) to elders (also of both sexes) is thus not a *class* subordination (which naturally does not make it any less significant). Again, a concept is lacking to pin down this phenomenon in a single word. Terray is therefore wrong when he states that, 'The relations of exploitation of the lineage mode ... bring forth social categories defined principally on the basis of age and sex: elders exploit cadets and men exploit women.'[14] In actuality the 'social categories' are prior: it is they that create the 'categories of exploitation' – the 'justifications' in other words, and the mechanisms, for that exploitation to take place. Additionally one should not forget that in the traditional Chinese lineage, older boys 'exploit' younger boys, older women younger women etc., in other words, the modalities of domination are numerous, but despite this 'alliances of classes' do occur – for example, between boys and girls of the same generation, but these alliances are *within* the ideology of kinship, or were rather until the old social order *as a whole* (not the lineage organization specifically) began to crack and polarise as the revolution began to get under way.[15]

We must thus direct back at Meillassoux and Terray an observation made by Godelier that (commenting on the enormous number of ethnographic cases now known to anthropologists)

> Given the sheer amount of this material we are understandably cautious and sceptical about the work of some anthropologists and philosophers of history who hastily erect one or two concrete cases as archetypes of the 'hunting mode of production' or the 'pastoralist mode of production' ... For in order to assert the existence of one or more modes of production specific to hunting and gathering societies (but not a 'hunting mode of production') *all* such societies must first of all be compared in order to determine whether the differences between them all belong to the same group of possible transformations (which at present we do not think is the case)[16]

and in this instance we obviously have in mind the fiction of the 'lineage mode of production'. The more interesting questions which Godelier goes on to pose are *why* in some societies one finds generation types of kinship systems, and in others lineage-dominated systems, and how some social segments lose equal access to common resources, and stratification and ultimately the State appear.[17] In his discussion of this Godelier raises certain possibilities, namely, that certain lineages gradually gain control over communal resources and then represent themselves as speaking for or personifying the 'common' interests of all the others that they in fact dominate. He overlooks another possibility however – that lineages (and in this case the Chinese lineage specifically) were a response to 'frontier' conditions, and the strength and dominance of the lineages is actually related to the *lack* of the State apparatus in the regions where they flourished (in south China interestingly enough – far from the centres of State control far away to the north).[18]

Godelier himself is thus sceptical about the concept of the 'lineage mode of production' and in fact points up the failure, up to this point, of the Marxist anthropologists to answer the central questions of kinship analysis, let alone the emergence of classes within such 'kinship' societies.[19] But at least the elements of such a theory become clearer when we examine specific cases – the sources of inequality in traditional Chinese society being in the

emergence of economic differentials, patriarchy, age and generational grading, progressive monopoly by the elders of ritual and
the ancestor cult and the making of such inequalities (or rather
their legitimation, since people were perfectly aware of them) by
a kinship ideology stressing orderly descent and the cohesion of
the social unit (in this case the lineage). This is basically a
structural question then, and reference to the historical origin of
the lineages, their technology and their relationship to agricultural activities, while of great interest, are really secondary.

There is nevertheless a strong tendency in the anthropological
literature to idealise the actual state of affairs, and the strongest
advocates of this are, not surprisingly, those who stress the
primacy of exchange over production. Undoubtedly the leading
representative of this school is Sahlins who says that, 'In the
course of primitive social evolution, main control over the
domestic economy seems to pass from the formal solidarity of the
kinship structure to its political aspect.' So far so good, but then
he continues,

> As the structure is politicized, especially as it is centralized in
> ruling chiefs, the household economy is mobilized in a larger
> social cause. This impulse transmitted by polity to production
> is often attested ethnographically. For although the primitive
> headman or chief may be himself driven by personal ambition,
> he incarnates the collective finalities, he personifies a public
> economic principle in opposition to the private ends and petty
> self-concerns of the household economy. Tribal powers that be
> and would-be powers encroach upon the domestic system to
> undermine its autonomy, curb its anarchy, and unleash its
> productivity.[20]

A positive assessment of the elders indeed! Sahlins in fact goes on
approvingly to quote a statement by Mary Douglas to the effect
that poverty is largely caused by lack of authority, in such a way
as to suggest that her comment on the Lele is to be taken as a
general rule. Sahlins subsequent comment is very revealing:
'The issue is between a chronic tendency to divide and disperse
the community, and, on the other side, the development of
political controls which would check this fission and effect an
economic dynamic more appropriate to the society's technical
capacity.'[21]

The respects in which Sahlins is mistaken here should be apparent from what we have already noted in this essay – the inherent tendency of lineage formations to 'divide and disperse' under the pressure of their own economic 'contradictions', on the one hand, and the concentration of political power to be the symptom and beginning of generational, economic and sexual stratification, on the other. Sahlins goes on to compound the error by remarking:

> The impact of the political system upon domestic production is not unlike the impact of the kinship system. But then, the organization of authority is not differentiated from the kinship order, and its economic effect is best understood as a radicalization of the kinship function. Even many of the greatest African chiefs, and all those of Polynesia, were not disengaged from the kinship nexus, and it is this which renders comprehensible the economics of their political acts – as well as the politics of their economics.

The supposed justification for this lies in a tautology that Sahlins puts forward as an explanation – that he is only talking about those societies 'where kinship is king and the "king" only a superior kinsman'.[22] In subsequent pages Sahlins continues in this vein, stressing continually the 'benevolent interest of the headman in the process of distribution', because 'kinship is a social relation of *reciprocity*, of *mutual aid*'.[23] Clearly the entire thrust of the French critique has bypassed Sahlins. The closest he comes is to note that kinship, thus conceived, functions as an ideology, and that 'everywhere in the world the indigenous category for exploitation is "reciprocity"'.[24] In part, this all arises from Sahlins' undefended belief that in 'kinship' societies 'transaction' (i.e. exchange) is 'more detached from production' than it is in modern industrial societies.[25]

All this naturally raises the fundamental, but not yet resolved, question of the relationship between kinship and the economy. The French Marxists clearly see the economy as prior, while Sahlins (and the Anglo-Saxon tradition generally) see kinship as prior in any explanatory or analytical scheme. Furthermore we have seen that a kinship analysis – whether offered by the anthropologist or as an indigenous folk model – can be a mystification. What then exactly is the status of kinship? Terray's comments on this are worth quoting at length; when he reflects on the inability of the analysis of kinship to reveal the fundamental structure of a whole society:

> In a more general way, the process of making kinship into a single theoretical entity seems to me to be no better than the invention of 'totemism' so justly condemned by Claude Lévi-Strauss: it brings together under one heading systems whose position and functions are not the same in every socioeconomic formation. Some of these systems organize social life as a whole, whole others affect only some sectors, and these again differ widely: in some cases it may be production, in others consumption, or in still others, marriage contracts. To give kinship studies a strategically decisive value for the understanding of primitive societies, 'kinship' must be understood as more than a simple combination of terms and attitudes, and kinship systems must be considered in their functional aspect as much as their formal aspect: at this point the unity of the entity 'kinship' can no longer be thought of as given and has to be proved.[26]

What is necessary, then, in the present case, is to see the ways in which the relations of production are based on genealogical kinship relations: the requirements of production and the requirements of reproduction (i.e. kinship) are inextricably linked (although we should also note here that kinship is more than reproduction – it is also security, power, status, psychological satisfaction and other things as well).

One of the interesting theoretical points to emerge from this is the evident fact that structurally similar kinship systems (in this case the patrilineage) can be found in conjunction with different systems of production and in different ecological settings. This does not necessarily imply, as some would suggest, that kinship is 'autonomous' and irreducible to production factors. What it does suggest is that there are only a relatively limited number of structural permutations which kinship systems can take (given the unchangeable biological factors which underlie all such systems) and that the specific 'choice' of system is a product of history and cultural decisions, as much as it is of ecology or of a particular mode of production (which, as we have stressed, is analytically independent of the kinship organisation). A Chinese lineage may thus practise rice farming, other grain (e.g. wheat) farming, fruit and vegetable growing, pastoralism, fishing or petty commodity production, or some combination of several of these, and possibly combining agriculture with trade and/or the restaurant business and even widespread migration of its (especially male) members abroad, while retaining the same structural kinship features. The *functions* of the lineage organisation itself may vary too: in some circumstances it may provide a hierarchical organisation of production relations for the essential benefit of the lineage elders, while in others (especially in 'frontier' conditions) it provides a relatively egalitarian organisation for appropriation of virgin land and a mechanism of co-operative work and produce sharing.

Kinship may thus function simultaneously as both infrastructure and superstructure (i.e. the juridical and ideological relations), in some cases as the dominant mode of the organisation of production itself, and in others as their ideological framework or justification. Kinship therefore does not just 'exist' – it exists because it performs functions. Neither kinship nor the economy are autonomous spheres but interpenetrate in a variety of (often complex) ways, including the characteristic way in which economic activities appear, or are made to appear, as an aspect of kinship. Kinship does not merely have a function in production, nor does it merely 'mask' actual relations of production. It may do both these things, while still retaining its status as a system of social organisation in and for itself.

Regarding the question of the existence of classes one may thus determine at least three stages: a stage in which kinship prevails as the chief mode (practical and ideological) of social organisation, and in which kinship *categories* exist, some of which are subordinated to others; a second stage of transition during the penetration of capitalism, when classes begin to appear in the wider society and are to some extent reflected in the lineage organisation – a stage when kinship still retains its ideological status although its practical significance is already becoming diminished; and a third stage when classes are well developed in the wider society and thus cut across kinship boundaries, which may still be retained, especially by the elders, as a mystification (a 'masking') of and justification for their class domination. The precise point reached in this historical process needs to be clearly defined before discussion about the existence of classes in kinship societies becomes relevant, otherwise it too exists in the much vilified 'ethnographic present' allegedly scorned by the Marxist anthropologists, although this is an error of which many of them are still guilty. A 'fetishism of production' is thus as much to be avoided as a 'fetishism of kinship'.

Kinship then is not 'outside' production: it is rather the social and ideological form through which it is realised. Its functions are multifaceted and will vary, for example, depending on whether or not there is an economic surplus. We can predict in the Chinese case that when there is no surplus (or a shortfall), kinship and economy function to form a more or less single unit, but when there is a surplus, the forces of fission and segmentation (which are essentially economic in nature) begin to appear – even though they may still be masked by the kinship ideology. When irrigation and other technological advances occur, vertical relations are likely to become intensified and stratification begins to become pronounced. But the status of the lineage *per se* in either case is not disturbed or questioned: it is still seen as the best way of organising labour and of promoting physical, economic and social security, as both an economic and a kinship unit. As Godelier phrases it, 'it is difficult to contrast economy and kinship as though they were two "institutions" with different functions'.[27] And as we have noted, and as Godelier likewise goes on to note, 'changes in the material base do not uniformly affect kinship relations – either the diverse elements which compose them or the discrete spheres of action which they organize'.[28] He continues:

> We are here clearly dealing with kinship relations that function simultaneously as infrastructure and superstructure. In effect they control the access of groups and individuals to the conditions of production and to resources, they regulate marriages (when demographic conditions permit), they provide the social framework of politico-ritual activity but they also function as an ideology, as a symbolic code for expressing relations between men, and between men and nature.[29]

But *why* kinship – as opposed to the political, or the religious, or some other sphere? Why is it so important? Godelier answers this as follows (and we would again go along with him here): '… kinship … must also function as the system of relations of production regulating the rights of groups and of individuals in respect to the means of production and their access to the products of their labour. It is because the institution functions as the system of relations of production that it regulates the politico-religious activities and serves as the ideological schema for symbolic practice.'[30] There is thus as Godelier points out a hierarchical arrangement of functions and structural causalities – and the effects that they have on each other and the arrangement of this hiearchy become the interesting questions. Form and function should not be disengaged from one another.

In the Chinese case too there is an important ethnographic dimension to this that we have not yet discussed. Generally, amongst typical peasants, the unit of production was small – it was the household (even though this might be organised on an extended basis) – and this was linked through markets and the sale of produce to merchants who accumulated on a larger scale. It was principally amongst the gentry families that the lineage was given great emphasis and priority, precisely in those conditions where the reproduction of the basic unit of production (the household) was not a problem, but where it was necessary to accumulate property and agricultural surplus, to acquire sufficient land to live on the rent, to perpetuate political influence and to maintain class status. In such a situation the lineage was actually used, if not 'created', for extra-kinship purposes – economic, political and educational (lineages often maintained their own schools, frequently with the intention of training their members' children to sit the Imperial examinations for entry to the state bureaucracy). Feuchtwang describes the system as follows:

> Lineage organization meant that inclusion in a lineage could give security of tenure on trust land to a member tenant and the right to send his children to its school for the few months when they might be spared from production. It might even mean the rare chance of leisure – class lineage managers deciding to sponsor a poor child for further education. These factors too were reinforcements to the hope of upward mobility for the peasant and meant his acceptance of descent organization, the norms of marriage, ancestor worship, and the attendant morality of filial piety, all beliefs to which the leisure class adhered as a necessary part of *their* strategy. Peasant producers, however, could only share these beliefs with a large number of

modifications in marriage and adoption customs, since they could not afford the excessive dowry system and other encumbrances involved in maintaining alliances and a line of descent. For the peasant producers such modifications resulted in a much narrower range of alliance. It was still a kinship-based organization and an ideology founded in agricultural production with all its concomitants of storage and continuity of a fixed means of production. However, it supported forms of political organization for a leisure class which were on a much wider scale.[31]

Because of the problems of maintaining landed property in the light of inheritance laws, and the desire to avoid the petty obligations of kinship and be near the main centres of accumulation, the rich, as Feuchtwang points out, tended to congregate in the towns, *which was precisely where the lineages were weakest*.[32] The lineage was thus not only agriculturally based, but was something that could be 'played' by the gentry-elders from a distance – from the towns. When a member of the gentry class could enter the bureaucracy, so much the better. He could then increase his opportunities to plunder through tax farms, corruption and similar devices, including the extension of political protection, bureaucratic positions as magistrate and participation in the state religion, which excluded the masses, but was nevertheless important to their identity reproduced through the ancestral structure.[33]

The existence of class relations in this case must not be confused with relations between the sexes, or even between the elders and juniors, but with the *separation* from the kinship unit of a group whose activities of appropriation and accumulation, although often disguised in kinship terms, actually rupture the essential requirements of co-operation and reciprocity required by the system and its ideology. Only then do *classes* (as opposed to stratificational categories of other kinds) appear: classes, that is, over and against kinship in reality and whose assimilation to the apparatus of the State becomes gradually more and more complete – in fact come eventually to be identified with it, indeed to *become* it. When this point is reached the accumulating classes actually find themselves (again in real terms) *opposed* to the kinship system and its demands (hence in part their movement to the towns) unless they can manipulate it in their own interest, especially by appealing to the kinship ideology and the idea of lineage solidarity while in fact violating these very principles. We must thus reject Terray's contention that 'in the lineage mode of production, women, youths, or whatever the category of persons occupying a definite position in the kinship system, may be regarded as constituting classes',[34] even if or when they are being exploited.

Indeed the absurd logic of this position is seen by Terray, although he draws the wrong conclusions from it: when, for example, he claims on the same page that if ego is 'exploited' as a son, he in turn 'exploits' as a father, maternal uncle, cross-cousin or whatever. The vacuousness of this concept of 'exploitation' is revealed by its infinite extension: 'The quarrels accompanying the transmission of inheritance and social privileges or witchcraft accusations may quite legitimately be interpreted as class conflicts.'[35] The fact that, even in Terray's own terms, such 'classes' never become conscious of themselves as classes is further evidence that they are *not* classes (except, as with 'exploitation', by some semantic or definitional sleight of hand, e.g. that they are 'formally' so).[36] What may happen, of course, is that *entire* lineages become aristocratic – a process of verticalisation occurs in which actual economic and political power is signalled by ritual and symbolic precedence (for example, in the state and ancestor cults).

Placing the debate in the somewhat different, although very interesting context of the evolution of the so-called 'Asiatic' social formations, Jonathan Friedman comments as follows:

The emergent structure, a quasi-sacred aristocracy, the conical clan-state can be found among the earliest Chinese states (Shang, Chou), which are similar to much-enlarged Kachin-type domains. These states, often considered feudal, are surely some of our best examples of the Marxist definition of the 'Asiatic' social formation. There is even evidence of the development of elaborate bureaucracies in these pre-irrigation states, i.e. long before supposed necessary by proponents of the hydraulic hypothesis. The doubling of genealogical ranking by an ordered series of administrative functions reinforces status differences with a largely imaginary division of labour, which tends to reduce competition by defining necessary functions for each segment in a larger bureaucratic entity. This is an

instrumental mechanism in the process whereby the exploitation of a community by a single lineage is expanded into class
exploitation. A sacred segmentary hierarchy whose function is
to control the reproduction of the society through its access to
the supernatural emerges as a class which is identical to the
state. The two phenomena are indistinguishable in 'Asiatic'
social formations.[37]

Class thus emerges *out of* not *within* the lineage formation, which is
not in any case, as we have argued, a 'mode of production'
anyway, which would be the proper nexus within which classes
might reasonably be expected to appear.

We see from this too that it is not simply a case of using
ethnographic examples to illustrate or demonstrate a theoretical
point: it is also the case that the theoretical enquiry itself greatly
illuminates and helps to structure the ethnographic data. It
shows, for example, how many variations there may actually be in
the 'model' or ideal–typical pattern of Chinese kinship, how class
differences effect these patterns, and how irrelevant the 'official
model' could be in the lives of many 'average' peasants. It would
take another essay to do so, but an interesting example that would
more fully illustrate this would be the resistance on the part of
many women to the patriarchal ideology, a resistance which took
a variety of forms including emmigration, the 'no-marriage
movement' in south China and strategies for attaining some
degree of economic independence amongst working women (and
virtually all non-leisure class women *were* workers). It likewise
helps to illustrate the ways in which the kinship principle
co-existed with other kinds of organisations – associations in
particular – although again these were often linked to kinship
(membership of clans, surname associations, many religious
organisations, etc. being through kinship), which in turn once
again illustrates the pervasiveness of the kinship ideology. The
idea of the State as an extended family, and which uses the
terminology and the structural principles of kinship to mobilise
and control its citizens, is a theme which appears constantly in the
literature on contemporary and post-revolutionary China –indi-
cating that amongst the masses, the ideology of kinship is
certainly not dead, even if its older-type manifestations seem to
have passed away.[38]

Finally, the questions we have raised here throw interesting light
on general explanations of traditional Chinese social structure,

and especially Karl Wittfogel's thesis of 'Oriental Despotism' – that Chinese society was ruled according to autocratic or despotic centralised principles which emanated from the State's monopoly of control over large-scale public enterprises and, in particular, irrigation.[39] In fact the kinship ideology and the actual territorial, political and economic power of the lineages (together with other geopolitical factors such as the distance between the more distant provinces and the capital) rendered this absolutist centrism impossible, despite the influence of the bureaucracy (which itself in practice had to come to terms with the powerful local lineages). Likewise, Wittfogel's attempt to show that class conflict was not a feature of Chinese society proves to be entirely untrue on closer analysis: the general thesis of monolithic despotism simply does not accord with the sociological facts, including the new well recognised one that the rulers of China had to accommodate themselves to the existing pressure groups in society – at various times the Taoists, the Buddhists, the gentry, the court eunuchs, the bureaucrats, the provincial warlords, and so on.[40]

In conclusion then, we are forced to modify radically, if not to reject altogether, the thesis of Meillassoux, Rey, Terray and others, that such a thing as a 'lineage mode of production', within which classes in any developed sense of the term occur, exists. There are many further details that could have been explored – the process of recruitment to these 'classes', succession to power and office, and so on. Part of the problem, as we have indicated, is the generalising from one or two cases to a universal theory. Marxist anthropology has clearly not moved beyond many examples of its non-Marxist counterpart in this respect, despite its scientific pretensions. What the French Marxists have undoubtedly done is to pose certain hypotheses, and quite rightly to draw attention to the very problematic status of kinship and to its relationships with the economic and political spheres. Much work of clarification remains to be done, nevertheless we can make a start, and the Chinese lineage, perhaps the world's most widespread example of patrilineal organisation, certainly seems as good a place to begin as any other.

NOTES AND REFERENCES

1. Georges Dupré and P. P. Rey, 'Reflections on the Pertinence of a Theory of the History of Exchange', *Economy and Society*, vol. 2, no. 2, 1973, p. 145.

2. John Clammer, 'Economic Anthropology and the Sociology of Development: "Liberal" Anthropology and its French Critics', in I. Oxaal, T. Barnett and D. Booth (eds), *Beyond the Sociology of Development* (London: Routledge and Kegan Paul, 1975), pp. 219–22.

3. Maurice Freedman, *Lineage Organization in Southeastern China* (London: Athlone Press, 1958), p. 69.

4. See Barbara Ward on this: 'Varieties of the Conscious Model: The Fishermen of South China', in M. Banton (ed.), *The Relevance of Models for Social Anthropology* (London: Tavistock Publications, 1969).

5. Including by Freedman himself in his later book on the subject: M. Freedman, *Chinese Lineage and Society* (London: Athlone Press, 1966), pp. 158–9.

6. Claes Hallgren, 'The Code of Chinese Kinship: A Critique of the Work of Maurice Freedman', *Ethnos*, vol. 44, nos 1–2, 1979.

7. See Hallgren, ibid., and Jack Belden, *China Shakes the World* (Harmondsworth, Penguin Books, 1973).

8. There are numerous studies of these groups. See, for example, Chang Chung-li, *The Chinese Gentry* (Seattle: University of Washington Press, 1955), and Morton H. Fried, *Fabric of Chinese Society: a Study of the Social Life of a Chinese Country Seat* (New York, 1969).

9. See Martin M. C. Young, *Chinese Social Structure: A Historical Survey* (Taipei: Eurasia Book Co. 1969), especially pp. 142–76.

10. For the best general account of the Chinese kinship system see Hugh D. R. Baker, *Chinese Family and Kinship* (London: Macmillan, 1979).

11. C. Meillassoux, *L'Anthropologie Économique des Gouro de Côte d'Ivoire* (Paris, 1964).

12. E. Terray, 'Historical Materialism and Segmentary-Lineage Based Societies', in his *Marxism and 'Primitive' Societies*, (New York: Monthly Review Press, 1972), p. 97.

13. Ibid., p. 101.

14. E. Terray, 'On Exploitation: Elements of an Autocritique', *Critique of Anthropology*, vol. 4, nos 13–14, 1979, p. 37.

15. For an acute literary analysis of this see Pa Chin's famous novel *Family*, of which there are many editions, the most recent being New York, Doubleday, 1972.

16. M. Godelier, 'The Appropriation of Nature', *Critique of Anthropology*, vol. 4, 13 & 14, 1979, p. 17.

17. Ibid., p. 23.

18. See Baker, *Chinese Family and Kinship*, pp. 153–9. See also M. Sahlins, 'The Segmentary Lineage: An Organization of Predatory Expansion', *American Anthropologist*, 63, 1961.

19. Godelier, 'The Appropriation of Nature', pp. 24–6.

20. Marshall Sahlins, 'The Domestic Mode of Production: Intensification of Production', in his *Stone Age Economics* (London: Tavistock Publications, 1974) p. 130.

21. Ibid., p. 131.

22. Ibid., p. 132.

23. Ibid., p. 133.

24. Ibid., p. 132.

25. Ibid., p. 187.
26. Terray, *Marxism and 'Primitive' Societies*, pp. 140–1.
27. M. Godelier, 'Modes of Production, Kinship and Demographic Structures', in M. Bloch (ed.), *Marxist Analyses and Social Anthropology* (London: Malaby Press, 1975), p. 4.
28. Ibid., p. 6.
29. Ibid., p. 10.
30. Ibid., p. 14.
31. Stephan Feuchtwang, 'Investigating Religion', in Bloch (ed.), *Marxist Analyses and Social Anthropology*, p. 75.
32. See Hugh D. R. Baker, 'Extended Kinship in the Traditional Family', in G. William Skinner (ed.), *The City in Late Imperial China* (Stanford: Stanford University Press, 1977).
33. Feuchtwang, 'Investigating Religion', p. 79 and M. Granet, *The Religion of the Chinese People* (Oxford: Basil Blackwell, 1975).
34. E. Terray, 'Classes and Class Consciousness in the Abron Kingdom of Gyaman', in Bloch, *Marxist Analyses and Social Anthropology*, p. 96.
35. Ibid., p. 96.
35. C.f. ibid., pp. 100–1.
37. Jonathan Friedman, 'Tribes, States and Transformations', in Bloch, *Marxist Analyses and Social Anthropology*, p. 195.
38. Baker, 1979, *Chinese Family and Kinship*, pp. 175ff.
39. K. A. Wittfogel, *Oriental Despotism: A Comparative Study of Total Power* (New Haven: Yale University Press, 1957).
40. For perhaps the most balanced critique and evaluation of Wittfogel's thesis see F. W. Mote, 'The Growth of Chinese Despotism: A critique of Wittfogel's theory of Oriental Despotism as applied to China', *Oriens Extremus* 8, 1961, pp. 1–41.

8 China and the 'Asiatic Mode of Production': An Inquiry

This chapter is an attempt to answer an empirical question – Why do the ideologues of the Chinese Peoples Republic reject as untenable the concept of the Asiatic Mode of Production (hereafter AMP)? – and in doing so to cast some much needed light not only on the question of the relevance of Marx's view for Asia, but perhaps as importantly, on *Asian* views of this relevance. We bring here into confrontation two interesting and very much opposed movements within contemporary Marxism – on the one hand, the recent extraordinary upsurge in interest in, and revival of, the concept of the AMP *in the West*,[1] and on the other hand, the complete rejection of this idea in China: physically the biggest and perhaps theoretically the most interesting country to have successfully carried out a revolution and established a social order which, it is claimed, are based on Marxist–Leninist principles. The reasons for the first factor – the revival of interest in the AMP – are various and include the desire to seek for connections between Marxism and the current underdevelopment debate, renewed interest in the attempt to bring Marxism and anthropology together by way of Marx's studies of pre-capitalist societies, and that fascinating cycle which seems to affect the social scientists of Europe – the perpetual falling out of fashion and then rediscovery of themes, theories and thinkers which have, so to speak, always been there. But the reasons for the other side of the equation – the Chinese rejection of the AMP – are not so well known, indeed one doubts if they are known at all to the present revivers of the AMP debate. Yet this is of tremendous importance: it tells us why the Chinese do not accept what some consider to be a major idea in Marx's thinking, and as such poses major questions for a rethinking of Marx in relation to Asia. We will proceed by way of a critical history of the evolution of Chinese thinking on this subject.

It is notable that one of the main sources of interest in the question of the AMP was *practice* (and not, as in the West, just theory). In addition, Marxist ideas about China were stimulated by the 1927 massacre and suppression of socialists by the Nationalist government. These events caused serious soul searching amongst Marxists as to whether the present catastrophe was caused by insufficient understanding of China's past, and how increased understanding of this past might lead to correct revolutionary action in the future. This immediately raised the question of the AMP: had China ever passed through a stage? had it been preceded by a period of slave society? or was China a *feudal* rather than an 'Asiatic' society?[2] The conclusion of the Marxists (whether trained in China, Russia or Japan) was that the AMP had never existed in China. The foremost spokesman for this view was Kuo Mo-jo who divided Chinese history into primitive-communal, slave, feudal and capitalistic periods, with a major social revolution marking the transition from each mode of production to its successor.

It is as a representative of this heterodox Marxist tradition that Mao Tse-tung must be seen. In the same year that the Nationalist purge of the communist movement took place, he published his famous 'Report on an Investigation into the Peasant Movement in Hunan'. In this, and in subsequent works, a number of unconventional ideas (from an orthodox Marxist point of view) were put forward, including the rejection of the necessity of a bourgeois revolution as the route to communism, the playing down of the role of the proletariat and the enhancement of the role of peasantry. In practical terms Mao arrived at these conclusions not by following orthodox doctrine, but through close empirical analysis of conditions in the Chinese countryside – of class divisions, forms of exploitation and issues of land reform. This empirical approach to social phenomena (whether contemporary or historical) was an important feature of the earlier stages of the Chinese assimilation of Marxism. Two features of the Maoist rejection of the AMP stand out: (i) the argument that *class* had always been a feature of Chinese society in historical times, and the corollary of this, that Marx's view of the self-contained and insulated village as a basis of 'Asiatic' society is illusory; and (ii) that *colonialism* and not the AMP was the other basis of Chinese 'underdevelopment' (the first being class domination and its accompanying exploitation.) Yet at the root of this there is also a paradox: that in rejecting the Eurocentric concept of the AMP, Mao merely embraced another, that of 'completely assimilating the country's historical phases to those of Europe – first slavery and then feudalism'.[3] This unilinear theory, however, does not appear very specific with regard to the actual nature of, for example, 'feudalism' in the Chinese context.

But why? Here several answers suggest themselves which seem to indicate a struggle between two rather contradictory but equally powerful tendencies: on the one hand, a desire to remain close to orthodox Marxist-Leninism (or at least as seen through the prism of Stalinism) and to represent China not as a unique or exotic case but as part of universal (and therefore unilineal) history; and on the other hand, the strong forces of nationalism, belief in the uniqueness, antiquity and continuity of Chinese culture, and emphasis not on the passivity, but on the revolutionary potential of the peasantry (in short on what the Russians rather like to call 'Han chauvinism'). This naturally leads to tension between a desire to be Marxist and a desire to express the deep belief in the special conditions of Chinese society. The tradition of empirical investigation earlier alluded to (and which has re-emerged strongly in recent years under the guise of 'investigation and research' and the 'four histories')[4] has only fuelled this by promoting explorations into questions of Chinese ethnic identity and territorial and cultural expansion, early trade, national minorities, major geographical and cultural differences within China and other such topics, all of which go against the static view of 'Asiatic' society. The emphasis is more on Chinese capacity for autonomous and indigenous change, *once* the shackles of colonialism without and landlord exploitation within have been thrown off. The current debate amongst western Marxists (for example, Melotti) about unilinealism versus multilinealism is really an attempt to grapple with this contradiction – between the universalist demands of the unilineal model of history and the particularistic impulses of pluralistic development models, which give Asia the 'right' to develop in ways which have nothing to do with western patterns.

Part of the problem here, of course, lies with the word 'Asiatic'. It needs to be remembered that Marx himself, Engels, Lenin, Trotsky and others even regarded pre-revolutionary Russia as 'semi-Asiatic'. In some uses of the term then Asiatic refers to a *mode of production*, in others it refers to its more usual geographical meaning. The two uses should not be confused, however, especially as yet another tension is likely to arise here: between those who reject the AMP because it is not part of the old unilinear scheme, and those who in their enthusiasm for the AMP make it a universal stage of history!

There are factors here too which cannot be fully explained by historical materialism. It is well known that Marx regarded the Asiatic communal form as stifling to human development, whereas he regarded the Germanic commune as containing the seeds of liberty.[5] This may well have seemed to be the case from Europe, but would it look like that from Asia? From a Chinese point of view and psychological perspective, certainly not. The pre-revolutionary 'commune' was not a perfect social organism, but it did evidently contain the seeds of liberty. What is partly wrong here is not only Eurocentrism, but the fact that Marx's seemingly historical analysis is actually ahistorical, collapsing as it does long periods of complex events into simple categories. It has not yet proved possible to find a scholar who can specify exactly *when* the AMP prevailed in China, when it arose and if and when it was succeeded or preceded by some other mode of production, despite the fact that so many western Marxists find it a suitable characterisation of Chinese history.

Certain anthropological assumptions are also made here about 'Asiatic' society – absence of private property, low level of production, lack of outside links, no internal contradictions that could give rise to endogamous development, etc, all of which are at best only partially true, and are in any case wild generalisations for an area as large and diverse as that of China. Above all, the theory that the State was despotic and all powerful in China is a travesty: the fact is that the *weakness* of the State is a key to a good deal of Chinese history, together with the idea not explored yet by Marxists, of *culture*. What has gradually emerged in the course of Chinese history, and which continues to bind together the whole idea of Chinese unity and identity, is the belief in a homogeneous and deeply rooted culture. It is this which enables Chinese to migrate without losing their identity, to assimilate other cultures (the Manchus for example), to cohere in times of extreme political instability and decentralisation, and so on. The *State* has always until recently played a minor role in this, despite its formal apparatus of administration, and traditional culture has proved one of the hardest nuts for the Chinese communists to crack (and they have not yet succeeded). This is precisely the factor that Wittfogel ignored to his cost in his massively misconceived theory of oriental despotism/hydraulic society. As a *culture* China is undoubtedly unique; but as a historical entity it is, of course, equally part of world history.

Part of the basis for the revival of the AMP then rests on a profound ignorance of Chinese history. Take, for example, the following statement of Melotti's: 'China can be called the most classic and significant example of a society based on the Asiatic mode of production, in that it achieves the fullest social development of any society so based. Moreover it did so without having any contacts with the rest of the world, not even those periodic relations with the West experienced by India and the Middle East back to Hellenic times at least.'[6] The first sentence is interesting: *how* then did China develop so fully on the basis of the static AMP – a question, of course, not answered. So is the second, since it reveals an ignorance so profound. China then had no contacts with the world! If none with India – where did Buddhism come from? If none with Europe – has Melotti (an Italian!) not heard of Marco Polo? Of Nestorian Christianity in China which dates from the sixth century? If none with Southeast Asia, what about the voyages of Cheng Ho in the fifteenth century? None with Northern Asia? with Mongolia? Korea? Japan? Even as late as the nineteenth century Melotti (and Marx) are singing the same tune. Melotti thus quotes Marx on the great Taiping rebellion: 'The only original thing about this Chinese revolution is its bearers. They are not conscious of any task except the change of dynasty. They have no slogans.'[7] This is breathtaking. The Taipings, profoundly influenced by quasi-Christianity brought to them from outside, set about attempting a total revolution in Chinese society, politics, morals and religion. One can see, of course, where this extraordinary logic and reading of history is leading: to the idea that the Maoist revolution is at base just another dynastic change! Again chronic Eurocentrism lies not far below the surface. According to Melotti there was no civil society in China (although his statements about the level of development of Chinese civilisation presumably contradict this). Most historians would regard Chinese civilisation as one of the most developed, if not the most developed in human history. And here Melotti quotes Gramsci: 'In the East State was all; civil society was a primordial and amorphous mass. In the West there was a

proper balance between State and civil society and through the
hazy outlines of the State one could immediately discern a rugged
structure of civil society.'[8]

Perhaps the root of this is to be found in a comment of Carrère
d'Encausse and Schram to the effect that, 'The major contradiction in Marx's thought regarding the non-European countries is
that between his rather narrow Eurocentrism on the cultural
level, and his worldwide vision on the strategic level.'[9] The result
of Marx's views on the 'Oriental heaven' and in particular its
absence of private property, its despotism and its isolated petty
commodity production was the conclusion that, 'The AMP was
regarded by Marx as a very early stage in the development of
humanity, growing directly out of primitive communism. To
declare that the Asian countries are still at a phase corresponding
to the dawn of civilization, and that they would never have
emerged from their stagnation without Western intervention, is to
condemn in advance any attempt by the peoples of these countries
to modernize while retaining their own personalities.'[10] The
Maoist appeal to the dignity of Chinese civilisation was a natural
reaction to this kind of attitude. It is of interest to note that in the
1930s the Chinese and Russian views of this coincided. At the
Leningrad conference of 1931 the AMP concept was dropped
from the official vocabulary on the grounds that it was simply a
variant of feudalism – largely on the ideological grounds of the
unity of the peoples of the East and the West and on the existence
of class struggles in early Asian history. As Carrère d'Encausse
and Schram also point out, the 'rediscovery' of the AMP was
made neither in China nor in Russia, but in Europe, by European
Marxists whose motives were at the best mixed – one being to
exalt classical antiquity at the expense of Asia.[11]

The reasons for the Chinese rejection of the AMP are thus fairly
easily stated. But with the current western anthropological
rediscovery of the concept we might also go on to draw some more
general conclusions from the way the Chinese would look upon
the AMP debate. (i) It helps us to explain why, with the
rediscovery of the AMP in Russia after about 1964, Marxism has
been so violently attacked as non-Marxist, revisionist, non-social-
ist, and chauvanistic by Soviet writers. The essential reason is the
Maoist claim to represent one in a range of models of socialism –
one expressing the specific uniqueness of Chinese traditions –
while yet claiming to be in the vanguard of revolution in the Third

World. The key corollary of this claim is, of course, the highly unorthodox rejection of the proletariat in favour of the peasantry.[12] (ii) We must also sympathetically consider the Chinese view that rather than proving to be a fruitful and exciting Marxist concept (such as that of class, or alienation), the AMP has proved to be a *barrier* to real research, by predefining the terms of the discussion. It has not even proved fruitful in the sense that the concept of feudalism so richly has. Indeed, this is clear if one looks at debates about the AMP by westerners: they revolve eternally around the same (and often semantic) issues. Rarely do they generate fresh research or serious historical or ethnological investigations. (iii) The Chinese rejection of the AMP is not merely a negative move, but redirects attention back to a much more fundamental Marxist concept – that of *class*. Mao from the beginning analysed China in class terms, a trend that has been paralleled by Soviet sinologues. The AMP is antithetical to a class analysis – the two cannot exist together. The rejection of the AMP is thus also a vindication of the validity and fruitfulness of class analysis and of a movement towards concrete studies of modes of exploitation. The AMP is far too generalised, ahistorical and abstract to make this possible. This in turn is tied up with the whole Chinese attitude to the so-called social sciences and their replacement of sociology, and to a much lesser extent anthropology (which are regarded, rightly no doubt, as 'bourgeois' subjects), with an indigenous tradition of social investigation incorporating Maoist study methods with empirico-historical research techniques.

We can go extending the list. (iv) The rejection of the AMP concept has important implications for the Chinese development model. Acceptance of the AMP would imply that the sources of change in Chinese society were wholly exogamous, whereas studies show quite clearly that the genius and patterns of the Chinese revolutionary pattern are in fact endogamous. Even Marxist-Leninism had to be nativised to make it acceptable and workable! (v) A Marxism freed from the ecocentrism that still marks so much of its provides the best, and perhaps at present, the only viable basis for a critique of *Orientalism* – the idealisation, abstraction and a historicism of much scholarship on the East. But to do this Marxism must first fully shake off its own nineteenth-century trappings and cultural baggage. If it cannot do this (and whether or not remains to be seen) it simply becomes (and in many cases has become an acute case of) Orientalism itself.[13] In a sense the Chinese experience represents both a practical and a theoretical refutation of Orientalism – a refutation which necessitates the abandonment of the AMP. As Turner puts it so well:

> The end of Orientalism requires a fundamental attack on the theoretical and epistemological roots of Orientalist scholarship which creates the long tradition of Oriental Despotism, mosaic societies and 'Muslim City'. Modern Marxism is fully equipped to do this work of destruction, but in this very activity Marxism displays its own internal theoretical problems and uncovers those analytical cords which tie it to Hegalianism, to nineteenth-century political economy and the Weberian sociology. The end of Orientalism, therefore, also requires the end of certain forms of Marxist thought and the creation of a new type of analysis.[14]

And this is certainly not the sort Melotti endorses in his praise of the decomposition of the AMP into the 'AMP proper', 'sub-AMP', 'para-AMP', etc.[15] Indeed the mania for classification (*except* where it is a preliminary and adjunct to explanation) is one of the first things that needs to go from the Marxist 'Methodology' if such it can yet be called.

In conclusion we can draw some general lessons from this whole discussion. The first of these is that the western Marxists' 'rediscovery of the AMP will prove to be a big mistake unless they can make it the springboard for a more genuinely non-Eurocentric, more Asia-centred (or Afro or Latin America centred) form, and internal critique, of orthodix Marxism. The lesson is: deviations are fruitful! This essentially argues against dogmatic, economistic, teleological, historist and Marxicological versions of Marxism: these are the real deviations. Conversely, it implies more empirical analysis, more willingness to consider those forces which have historically proved to be creative (e.g. the peasantry) regardless of whether or not they appear in the orthodox canon, more willingness to explore dynamic concepts such as culture and ethnicity (and to subject them to critical scrutiny), and more willingness to explore and admit the historical specificity of local conditions. One move that has been made in the latter direction, for instance, is the development of the idea of the articulation and co-existence of several modes of production in a given concrete social formation.

In the last analysis, then, a discussion about the Chinese attitude to the AMP has a much wider, indeed universal, significance, since it raises the whole enormous question of the relationship between western concepts and Asian societies. By looking at the problem from, for once, the Asian end, one realises that there is a point of view here that cannot be ignored, or dismissed, or simply classified as 'revisionist' (which in any case implies a quasi-sacred status for Marx's writings, quite antithetical to the spirit in which he wrote them). The Chinese case offers a profound challenge to the Marxist anthropology of the West, while simultaneously fulfilling in practice much of the programme of that anthropology, and especially the accomplishment of *praxis*, indigenisation, class analysis and so on, and even, although this too is not yet recognised in the West, the depth of scrutiny that Firth, for example, evidently feels is a unique characteristic of the Euro-American anthropological tradition.[16] In this respect we might follow the conclusion of Carrère d'Encausse and Schram that whereas in 'official' Marxism the problem is that of applying Marxism *to* Asia, in the Chinese view the issue is rather that of Marxism *in* Asia – 'the adaptation of Marxism to Asian conditions by the Asians themselves, not only in order to find new techniques for seizing power, but with the aim of breaking new paths in the revolutionary transformation of society' – which issue has now become *the* central issue.[17] And ultimately this is exactly what the AMP debate boils down to.

NOTES AND REFERENCES

1. Some leading examples being A. Bailey and J. R. Llobera (eds), *The Asiatic Mode of Production: Science and Politics* (London, 1980); M. Sawer, *Marxism and the question of the Asiatic Mode of Production* (The Hague, 1977); L. Krader, *The Asiatic Mode of Production* (Assen, 1975); U. Melotti, *Marx i il Terzo Mondo* (Milan, 1972) (English translation: *Marx and the Third World*, 1977). There are many others.
2. For a brief discussion of this debate and its context see Siu-lun Wong, *Sociology and Socialism in Contemporary China* (London, 1979).
3. Melotti, *Marx and the Third World*, p. 9.
4. Wong, *Sociology and Socialism in Contemporary China*, chapters 3 and 5.
5. E.g. Marx's essay, 'The British Rule in India', *New York Daily Tribune*, 25 June 1853 and Engels in *Anti-Dühring*.
6. Melotti, *Marx and the Third World*, p. 105.

132   *The Neo-Marxist Challenge and Renewal*

7. Melotti quoting Marx, ibid., p. 108.
8. A. Gramsci, Note on Machiavelli, quoted by Melotti, ibid., p. 103.
9. Helene Carrère d'Encausse and Stuart R. Schram, *Marxism and Asia* (London, 1969), p. 7.
10. Ibid., pp. 8–9.
11. E.g. Ferenc Tokei, 'Le mode de production asiatique dans l'oeuvre de K. Marx et F. Engels', *La Pensée*, 114, 1964. The work of Perry Anderson also approaches this genre.
12. For a very good study of this interplay of Russian and Chinese attitudes see E. Stuart Kirby, *Russian Studies of China* (London, 1975).
13. For support for this see Bryan S. Turner, *Marx and the End of Orientalism* (London, 1978).
14. Ibid., p. 85.
15. Melotti, *Marx and the Third World*, p. 74.
16. Raymond Firth, 'The Sceptical Anthropologist? Social Anthropology and Marxist Views on Society', in Maurice Bloch (ed.), *Marxist Analyses and Social Anthropology* (London, 1975). He should read Wong (op. cit.) with some care and keep in mind that social investigation in a revolutionary situation does not have quite the same presuppositions and *intentions* as conventional anthropological researches.
17. Carrère d'Encausse and Schram, *Marxism and Asia*, p. viii.

Part III
Areas of Application

9 Inequality and the Peasant Mode of Production: Theories of Production, Distribution and Ideology

The 'rediscovery' of the peasantry as a socio-economic category of major global importance has been seen by some as one of the most significant events in the recent history of the social sciences.[1] It is now widely recognised that the bulk of the world's rural population (and therefore the bulk of its total population) are 'peasants', and that this enormous group of humanity is by no means a passive and homogeneous rural proletariat, but has proved itself, on the contrary, to be a diverse and politically active force – as evidenced by the successful peasant revolutions of East and Southeast Asia, and the less successful but not necessarily less significant peasant movements in South Asia, Latin America, Africa and even Europe (where many people had forgotten that peasants still existed at all).

But what is a peasant? Does this enormously wide-ranging category contain within itself sufficient generalisable properties, despite geographical and cultural variation, to allow a universalisable definition to be made? This question and its implications are the basic themes of this chapter. In detail the question resolves itself into two problems – (i) can we provide a general working definition of a peasant mode of production? and (ii) can we regard such peasant social formations as autonomous, or are they essentially a product of underdevelopment, i.e. do they always stand in a relationship of structural dependency with their wider social setting (and/or the international economic system) in which their role is subordinate? The logical point with which to

135

begin this discussion is by examining briefly the concept of a mode
of production.

MODES OF PRODUCTION

The concept of a mode of production is a complex one, but more
because of its history than for analytical reasons.[2] My purpose
here will be simply to give a working definition that can be
employed in the analysis of the central questions of this paper.

A simple definition or description of an economic 'type', e.g.
'capitalism' or 'entrepreneurship', does not qualify as the concept
of a mode of production. Neither is a mode of production merely
the activities of production in themselves, e.g. hunting, farming,
since the concept also requires the addition of the *relations of
production* involved and the ideological and politico-juridical
superstructures which provide its context.[3] In a somewhat
different form this is expressed by Hindess and Hirst in the
statements that

> Now the concept of mode of production as an articulated
> combination of relations and forces of production precludes the
> construction of the concept of a particular mode of production
> by means of the simple juxtaposition of a set of relations and a
> set of forces. On the contrary the concept of a particular mode of
> production is the concept of a determinate articulated combi-
> nation of relations and forces of production. This means that
> there can be no definition of the relations or of the forces of
> production independently of the mode of production in which
> they are combined.[4]

This follows from their succinct definition of a mode of
production: 'A mode of production is an articulated combination
of relations and forces of production structured by the dominance
of the relations of production. The relations of production define a
specific mode of appropriation of surplus-labour and the specific
form of social distribution of the means of production corresponding to that mode of appropriation of surplus-labour.'[5]

This definition, as a general one, allows for there to be varieties
of modes of production, e.g. the capitalist one in which the
capitalists buy labour from the workers, who must sell their

labour-power in order to buy the means of subsistence, and for there to be varieties of the forces of production etc. without the specific mode of production collapsing. Any particular mode of production is part of a 'social formation' – the wider political, ideological and social network of which it is an essential part. As we now well know, a single social formation may contain more than one mode of production, although we must also remember that modes of production and social formations must be kept conceptually distinct. On the basis of this preliminary definition (which will necessarily be further refined as we proceed), we can move towards the central question: is there a 'Peasant Mode of Production'?

THE STRUCTURAL CHARACTERISTICS OF PEASANT SOCIETIES

To answer this question requires, first of all, a discussion of the 'typical' (if there be such a thing) characteristics of peasant economies and societies. Are there indeed such general features, or has the social scientist been led to see them by the belief that the category 'peasant' must imply some high degree of unity amongst its members? Or to put it another way, to what extent is the category of the 'peasant' an ideological rather than an empirical category? Here we should rightly fall back upon Shanin's very pertinent observation that 'a sociological generalization does not imply a claim of homogeneity, or an attempt at uniformity',[6] but rather that a comparative view requires the recognition of different historical and cultural contexts; of differences as well as similarities. Even as this is true at the empirical level of the sociological characteristics of peasant groups, it is also true at the interpretative level as well. Thus while a Marxist may see peasants as an exploited vestige of pre-capitalism, others may see them as a residual social category to be classified along with 'primitives', 'hunter-gatherers', etc., or as lying at one end of Redfield's famous (or perhaps notorious, in view of all the misleading thinking that it has given rise to) rural–urban continuum. The general change in point of view from thinking of peasants as an inert social mass to becoming a revolutionary vanguard in the 'Third World' has if anything added to the general confusion.

Shanin's solution to this is to produce a delimitation of the peasantry in terms of four factors: (i) the peasant family farm as the basic unit of multidimensional family organisation; (ii) land husbandry as the main means of livelihood directly providing the major part of consumption needs; (iii) specific traditional culture related to the way of life of small communities; (iv) the underdog position – the domination of the peasantry by outsiders.[7] These points require a certain amount of expansion as they raise issues about the generic form of peasant societies, and also some controversial questions. The question of generic forms I will pass over as quickly as possible so as to return to the central analytical problems of this paper.

The generic view contains a number of themes, which I will briefly enumerate. (1) The peasantry is both an economy and a society, in the sense that it is an entity based upon small-scale, largely low technology farming of landed property either owned or rented, and that the unit of the exploitation of this land is an individual family, linked through kinship with other virtually identical families, and who employ outside labour (or themselves work elsewhere than on their own land) only in rare and usually unavoidable circumstances. The household or family unit which is the focus of the peasant system is usually highly cohesive, acting as it does as an economic, domestic and even political unit. It is, of course, precisely these characteristics which give rise to the outsider's view of the peasant family as 'closed', authoritarian (even if benevolently so), conservative, suspicious of outsiders (and especially non-peasants), lacking in willingness to innovate, but very hardworking and engaged in an economy which fully utilises all available labour in whatever ways are appropriate. The large size of many peasant families is a function of this: where there are more members there is more labour, and hence higher productivity and greater security.

(2) A peasant family does not exist in isolation – it is linked with others in hamlets, villages and often in communal working units which may be based upon locality (i.e. residence), kinship or the necessity of performing certain communal tasks which, if neglected, damage the economic viability of the district as a whole (e.g. maintaining roads, paths, watercourses and irrigation works). Such tasks may be spontaneously performed, or may be undertaken at the instigation of governmental or other agencies. One should not overestimate the degree of co-operation or

communalism which exists – since such as there is often reflects only temporary utilitarian requirements and not any developed corporate sense – often extending no farther than ones hamlet, village quarter or even family or lineage.[8] It is from these characteristics that the 'classical' view of 'peasant culture' has emerged, which (except to a few Russian romantics of the last century) is usually uncomplimentary and represents the peasant as clannish, custom-ridden, non-innovative, with a very narrow range of loyalties. Culture itself is thus seen as 'traditional' in its nature – oral, simple in art and technology, lack of wide cultural (or for that matter geographical) horizons, lack of interest in education except that of a purely utilitarian kind, the prevalence of a 'folk culture' characterised by anonymity of its products, its transmission without major changes from one generation to the next, widespread existence of belief in magic (and possibly also of witchcraft), and intense suspicion of anything novel or foreign, which has been enshrined in Foster's famous concept of the 'image of the limited good'.[9]

A PEASANT MODE OF PRODUCTION?

On the basis of this brief discussion of the view taken by many writers on the generic characteristics of the peasantry, we can move to the first of our two central analytical questions: is there such a thing as a peasant mode of production? (I should add here in parenthesis that there is an issue raised by the foregoing discussion – which is the question of to what extent peasants do invariably share the characteristics often so readily ascribed to them. There are after all those who have noted the extreme resilience of peasant cultures, their economic efficiency in their own terms, the strength of character of their members, etc. If this were not so, one would have to side with Marx's unfavourable view of the peasantry against Mao's – and history has conclusively proved who was correct. My own view is that many of the objective structural characteristics of the peasantry (including their generally depressed status) have misled many observers into a falsely subjectivist position about the quality of peasant life. To anthropologists, which includes myself, all cultural types are methodologically and theoretically equal – primitives as much as proletarians – and peasants are no exception to this rule.)

To return then to the main question – are the definable characteristics of peasant economies sufficient to qualify them as a mode of production? The answer may be in the affirmative provided that we agree to regard the notion of the peasantry as a generic category, or to put it in Weberian terms, as an ideal type. What we must then explore is the particular (and unique) form of the combination of the relations and forces of production, the social distribution of the means of production, the mode of appropriation of surplus-labour and the articulation of these features with the social formation of which they are a part, which characterise the peasantry as an economy. Before we do so, we should again recall the point raised in the introduction that a mode of production is a *structural entity* within which there may be variations in, say, the forces of production, as indeed there presumably are between the Chinese, Malay, Tanzanian and Bolivian peasantries. The advantage of pursuing (at least at this stage in a heuristic way) a mode of production analysis is that it allows us to move away from dealing with mere sociological generalities (and the attendant widespread empiricist belief that a single counter-example destroys the generalisation's which it does not,) to a structural and conceptual approach from which it is possible to develop a genuine comparative model.

We may begin with a thumb-nail sketch of the peasant mode of production: it is that particular combination of primary, small-scale and low technology farming that is pursued through the total utilisation of the domestic labour power of the household which is the primary unit of production and consumption, and within which division of labour takes place on a functional basis, and the means of production are owned by the domestic unit itself and distributed amongst its members as their economic roles require. If any appropriation of surplus-labour takes place, it is through corvée or other communal co-operative projects, except in a feudal or certain socialist systems where the labour is devoted to the landlords or to State directed enterprises (e.g. the collective farm). In practice this definition is likely to need qualification in one very important respect – that although the tools of production may be owned by the productive unit itself (i.e. the peasant family), the basic resource upon which the entire system depends – land, may not be. An important distinction must thus be made between peasants who are owner-occupiers of their land and those who are tenants, squatters or in some other way utilising land not owned by themselves. In either situation there is in any case a tendency for landlords to enter into a relationship of exploitation with their peasant tenants, either directly through the charging of high rents or the expropriation of part of the product, or indirectly by debt-bondage resulting from the landlord's monopoly over provision of credit, fertiliser, etc., or through control of essential resources such as irrigation or facilities for rice-milling or marketing of produce. This, of course, is a *tendency*, not an invariable rule. The key factor in this characterisation of the peasant mode of production is not the structural description itself, but the question of its articulation (to use the fashionable word) with other modes of production which may co-exist with it, and with the social formation as a whole of which it is a part. It is precisely this feature which raises the second of our two analytical questions: do peasant modes of production always stand in a relationship of exploitation to the other modes of production/social formations with which they are associated? In fact, our two central questions are not really separate questions at all, as by now should be apparent, since we could actually rephrase them into a single question: is the peasant mode of production one which by definition is exploited?

In a hypothetical society in which peasants were the only inhabitants such a question could not arise, but in actual fact, both historically and in the contemporary world, peasants do not find themselves in this situation. On the contrary, they are generally to be found as one social component amongst others in complex societies containing not only peasants, but also large farmers, merchants, urban proletariats, rural aristocracies, urban middle classes, military élites, foreign industrial capitalists, plantation owners and landless labourers, intelligensias and even large tribal, nomadic or somewhat quaintly named 'analytically marginal groups' such as squatters, kibbutzniks or their own kind in some sort of semi-urbanised and/or proletarianised state. This phenomenon is nowadays somewhat more elegantly conceptualised as the 'co-existence of modes of production', and it is to this that we must now turn.

THE PEASANT ECONOMY: RELATIONS OF DOMINATION, EXPLOITATION OR AUTONOMY?

One of the implications of the preceding discussion is that we should regard the peasant economy as one *sui generis*, and not as

merely a point on an evolutionary continuum or a folk–modern
axis (i.e. Redfield), or as an incipient form of capitalism (Marx),
or, as is an increasing tendency recently, as a form, product or
symptom of underdevelopment (i.e. a type of 'informal sector' or
temporary petty-commodity production). There are certain
elements of truth in all these positions, but none of them
(individually or indeed taken together) provide a fully adequate
conceptualisation of the concrete nature of the peasant economy
as a general category. This is particularly the case when we
recognise that in many subtypes of the peasant economy we are
not dealing with a form of capitalist economy at all, but rather
with the situation familiar to many economic anthropologists that
Sahlins has dubbed the 'Domestic Mode of Production', an idea
in many respects inspired by the work of the Russian rural
sociologist A. V. Chayanov.[10] We must always bear in mind the
characteristics of the peasantry as a system of production *and*
distribution that we have already discussed.

But while it is true that these constitute the necessary
conditions for the existence of a peasantry, they do not constitute
the sufficient conditions. If a peasant economy co-exists with other
modes of production, this presupposes a context in which this
co-existence takes place – towns, other economic systems
(whether agricultural, e.g. commercial plantations, or industrial), and above all the apparatus of the State, including the
bureaucratic and administrative structures, systems of taxation
and social control, etc. Our hypothetically autonomous peasant
economy is in practice heavily influenced and modified by the
existence of these outside factors. The general categories of this
modification I will now attempt to list. (We should also note that
under the historical and contemporary feudal systems and under
what Marx would have called the 'Asiatic Mode of Production'
similar factors also obtain.)

1. Corvée or forced labour for the State, or for the feudal
   landlord (i.e. serfdom in the latter case), or military conscription.
2. Direct or indirect taxation.
3. Creation of a predominantly cash/consumer economy in
   which the peasant is obliged to sell his products on the market
   for money with which to obtain either necessities which he
   cannot produce for himself or acquire through barter, or

luxuries which he now desires or believes that he needs. This is the principle now generally called by Marxists the 'penetration of the capitalist economy (or mode)', and by non-Marxists the 'spread of the market principle'. Whatever the phrase the effect is the same – to draw the peasant's self-sufficient economy into a sphere where it is no longer self-sufficient.

4. 'Rationalisation' by the landlord of landed property – such as the European enclosure movement – which forces the peasantry either right off the land altogether or turns them into landless wage-labourers on the estates, farms or plantations of the landlords.

5. Debt-bondage – such as loaning peasants money against the security of their next harvest at very high rates of interest; paying for services in kind rather than cash, e.g. by coupons which can only be redeemed at the landlord's stores; fixing of prices for produce in return for undertaking processing (e.g. rice-milling) and/or marketing.

6. Urbanisation and the shift of the 'centre of gravity' from the rural to the urban sectors, both economically and psychologically.

7. Industrialisation, whether capitalist or socialist, which generates a need for a proletariat – often drawn from the land – and mechanisation and industrialisation of agriculture itself, which renders peasant farming less and less viable.

8. Colonialism, whether 'external' by a foreign power, or 'internal' (as for example in South Africa),[11] where the native peasantry are drawn into a commercial and usually export-oriented economy from which they not only do not benefit, but from which they may suffer an actual decline in their quality of living.

9. 'Political modernisation', whether it takes the form of massive state intervention in the natural economy (as under socialism) or the emergence of local bourgeois élites, no less oppressive and rapacious than their colonial predecessors, and characteristic of many modernising Third World countries.

No doubt this list is not entirely exhaustive, but it does represent the main processes of penetration of the wider social context into the peasant economy.

The general lesson is certainly clear – that an individual community, or in this case category of community, can only be understood through an analysis of *both* its internal structural characteristics and its relationship to the wider system. The key question then becomes that of whether this relationship is one of equality or dependency, and if of dependency, whether this involves benevolent co-operation or exploitation. It is for this reason that, contrary to the belief held by Radcliffe-Brown, the proliferation of individual ethnographic studies of peasant communities will not lead to a general picture of how the system works. Such a picture can only be arrived at by discovering the structural principles at work: the individual descriptive accounts then stand as illustrations of these principles. It is the manner of the integration of the peasant community into the wider system that is the main focus of interest, and in particular the processes by which the peasantry tends to get forced into an increasingly marginal situation in the overall social formation, especially 'in the sense that the juridical institutions, elaborated for the regulation of the great property, offer instruments which are much too unwieldly or otherwise unsuited to the regulation of small properties, and consequently give place to custom and illegality'.[12]

As we have indicated above, it is not so much that juridical institutions in themselves are the *cause* of increasing peasant incorporation into the wider (capitalist or socialist) social structure, but rather that they reflect this incorporation by providing the legal means by which the State and/or landowners can control and direct the economic processes and the access of the peasantry to material, legal or political resources. The intensification of relationships between the rural sector and the urban centres is usually an important aspect of this, with consequences not only for the economic linkages involved, but also for values, the social structures of the agrarian communities, and cultural goals, all of which suffer disruption. This disruption, of course, need not be negative: the spread of literacy, for instance, can throw open hitherto closed peasant communities and give them the very means of self-determination and control over resources of knowledge and communication which were denied them in their former state of social unselfconsciousness.[13]

The process of modernisation is thus a two-edged sword – it creates new and formerly unforeseen possibilities, new techniques of production, the possibility of education, politicisation and wider horizons, but at the cost of the breakdown of the traditional community, its family norms and many of its spontaneous cultural manifestations. Pearse summarises these processes under three general subtypes:

> *In the economic dimension*: movement from family-bound production towards productive enterprises largely dependent on industrial inputs.
>
> *In the structural dimension*: movement from membership of a neighbourhood community marked by 'structural peninsularity' towards membership of a national class-society.
>
> *In the cultural dimension*: movement from territorially defined cultural variety towards national cultural homogeneity modified by sub-cultural class-differentiation.[14]

The emergence of 'marginal' peasants – peasant-workers, agricultural wage-labourers, peasants organised into communes and collective farms, 'peasants in cities',[15] estate-workers, etc. – is an almost (if not always) inevitable consequence of these processes.

What we see there then is a very clear and historically well-validated process at work – the progressive incorporation of the peasantry into the complex structures of the modernising technico-industrial State. Given the kinds of linkages that we have discerned between the rural (peasant) and urban (industrial) sectors, we are at least in one sense justified in talking about this as a relationship of dependency. The peasantry, which may begin as a relatively autonomous form of natural economy, is increasingly drawn into structural dependence on the institutions – political, economic, juridical, psychological, technological and even cultural – of the industrial sector (even though, in terms of numbers of individuals, the rural sector may still well outstrip the urban – industrial). There is, however, a dimension of this equation which is frequently forgotten: in a very real and critical material sense the urban–industrial sector is ultimately dependent on the rural – where its food comes from. A hidden dimension of this rural–urban struggle is actually the way in which the industrial sector increasingly attempts either to minimise its independence on its *own* rural hinterland – by importing food from someone else's, or by developing synthetic proteins – or to control that hinterland by extending the scope of industrial–mechanised farming at the expense of traditional peasant methods, or, at the very least, to regulate the rural sector *from* the urban sector by monopolising procedures of 'planning' and 'environmental control' (none of which incidently were needed until the industrial sector began its depredations).

So if we speak of dependency as characterising the relationship of peasant economies to the wider society, does this imply that this relationship is also one of exploitation? It is probable that in no historical or contemporary society have the peasantry ever been in anything other than a subordinate position (cultural, psychologi-cal, political, as well as economic), which includes those societies such as China where a 'peasant revolution' has taken place. In the case of China (and no doubt in other examples as well) this concept of a peasant revolution is largely an ideological one, since while there is no doubt that the peasants played a major part in the execution of the revolution, this did not lead to their seizure of the sources of political, economic and social power. Indeed, they still remain at the bottom of the social and economic ladder.[16] This is not, of course, to deny their seminal role in the genesis and evolution of modern revolutions, but one doubts if any serious observer would claim that a genuinely 'peasant state' or a turning back of the universal processes of modernisation has ever occurred as a result of peasant-based social upheavals.[17]

But to return to our original hypothesis: dependency in itself need not necessitate exploitation. Dependency can be benign and even desired by the dependent (or both) parties in the relationship. A peasantry is exploited in so far as its material, cultural and psychological resources are extracted from it against its will and to its detriment: it is, in other words, the function of a particular relation of production, not *within* the peasant society itself (although exploitation may also exist in that context), but between the peasant society and the wider one with which it is enmeshed. It is the process of the incorporation of the peasant economy into the wider one, then, which is the root cause of potential exploitation of the peasantry. Whether or not this exploitation actually occurs, and the forms that it takes when it does, is a matter for concrete sociological and historical analysis to explicate for us.

SOME CONCLUDING REMARKS

We should not necessarily draw a pessimistic conclusion from any of the foregoing. Peasants are still a major proportion of mankind, they have been around for a long time, and it is probable that they will be with us for some considerable time to come. Indeed, if some analysts are correct, they will still be about long after the present industrial–urban–technological civilisation has brought about its own demise. Peasants have shown themselves, contrary to the popular image of them as dull-witted, to be constantly able to adapt, to find mechanisms for equalising some kinds of economic inequalities, to indulge in political resistance, etc. Rational economic planning at a national level also quite clearly indicates the importance of sustaining the rural sector, improving productivity, conditions of life and opportunities for rural dwellers, and avoiding those very factors of rural underdevelopment – poverty and cultural deprivation – which fuel peasant discontent. Even the idea of *re-establishing* the natural economy has come to be seriously proposed as a development strategy by some authors.[18] The educational strategies of Paulo Freire and those who follow his lead also point to directions which peasant communities might fruitfully follow. The category of the peasant economy is thus by no means historically exhausted (or theoretically exhausted for that matter, judging by the liveliness of continuing debate on the subject).

The sociological tradition of peasant studies, however, has generated a set of issues to which we should at least draw some attention. I would divide these issues into five main categories, which will be briefly described.

(i) The 'resistance to change' theory, or, 'why do peasants prove unco-operative in the face of development efforts?' Are there general principles underlying peasant unco-operativeness? Are the factors impeding innovation cultural – a product of the peasant value-system – or do they result from economic judgements made by peasant farmers according to a system of economic rationality not yet fully understood by development economists? (although some, such as Chayanov and Sahlins, the latter with his theory of the 'Domestic Mode of Production', have begun an attempt to do so). On the other hand, when peasants *do* prove to be responsive to innovations and opportunities, why is *this* so? How do 'attitudinal' explanations fit with those which allow precedence to the articulation of the peasant economy with the wider economy? Do constraints to development lie at the local or national levels? Is the problem essentially psychological, sociological, economic or political? A great deal of the literature on the peasantry deals essentially with these kinds of questions, but frequently without specifying the premises upon which their various arguments are based.[19]

(ii) The analysis of linkages between different modes of production when several of them co-exist within the same general social formation. How are surpluses expropriated at the local level? What are the relationships of power also at the local level? Who are the social brokers and how do they operate? How useful is the 'metropolitan-satellite' model in explaining not only relationships between countries, but also between social systems in the same country? This in practice becomes a question of the generation of a model of the articulation of modes of production and the development of empirical analyses based upon this model.[20]

(iii) The extent to which the peasant economy is characterised by petty-commodity production and by specific relations which are associated with this form of production. A related question is to what extent the peasantry are being increasingly forced into the role of what has now come to be known as the 'informal sector', that is, an informally organised fringe economy based on part-time and sometimes even unlicenced and illegal economic activities.[21] Important here is the role of the penetration of the capitalist economy, and of the political dimension of neo-colonialism and its role in perpetuating the social structures of underdevelopment.[22]

(iv) The ideological aspect of the term 'peasantry' must also be recognised, and in particular the dangers of developing *a priori* definitions of the term containing unwarranted cultural and psychological assumptions, which frequently have the effect of reducing the peasant to the role of the 'other' – an inarticulate and passive recipient of the advice of development 'experts', and the unwilling or unwitting tool or victim of other people's political and economic ambitions.[23]

(v) The importance of the political role of the peasantry in any of the primarily agrarian societies of the 'Third World' – in other words, in nearly all of them. Even in the industrialised world (both East and West) the peasantry is by no means a political factor to be ignored (as recent experience in Japan clearly reveals).

The study of the peasantry is thus very much a multidisciplinary one. It calls upon economics, sociology, anthropology, political science and psychology, and makes heavy demands on critical theory in all these fields. For, as we have seen, the problem of defining a peasant is not a simple descriptive problem – it is also very much an ideological one. We might well close with a quotation from Shanin:

> The emotional tension underpinning ambiguous contempt or utopian praise, the replacement of definition by allegory, as well as acute shortcomings in the conceptual grasp of the peasantry, were only too strongly felt in the Western intellectual tradition. The neglect of the study is but a symptom of this. It calls for a serious study, in the field of the sociology of knowledge, of the *eidos* of intellectual image-makers when dealing with a 'class that represents the barbarism within civilization' (Marx and Engels, *Selected Works*, Vol. 1, London 1950, p. 159). The treatment of peasant action as an 'undecipherable hieroglyphic to the understanding of the civilized' (Marx and Engels, ibid. 159) seemed to be determined by a conglomeration of factors, of which one stands out as crucial. The peasantry does not fit well into any of our concepts of contemporary society. This 'maddening' peasant quality seems to lie at the roots of the problems of research in this field.[24]

This is true, but the conceptual tools to deal with this problem now lie to hand; and the importance of dealing with the issue is not a merely theoretical one, although the practice and action must be based squarely on sound theory and sound analysis.

NOTES AND REFERENCES

1. For example by Teodor Shanin in the collection of readings edited by himself – *Peasants and Peasant Societies* (Harmondsworth: Penguin Books, 1971), p. 11.
2. See T. Asad and H. Wolpe, 'Concepts of Modes of Production', *Economy and Society*, 5, 1976. There are no doubt those who would disagree with me on this point. Readers with sufficient energy are referred to the two works by Barry Hindess and Paul Q. Hirst, *Pre-Capitalist Modes of Production* (London:

Routledge and Kegan Paul, 1975), and *Modes of Production and Social Formation* (London: Macmillan, 1977).

3. For a brief discussion of these issues and of some of the fallacies which arise from not making these distinctions, see J. Clammer, 'Economic Anthropology and the Sociology of Development', in I. Oxaal, T. Barnett and D. Booth, (eds), *Beyond the Sociology of Development* (London: Routledge and Kegan Paul, 1975), pp. 223 ff.

4. Hindess and Hirst, *Pre-Capitalist Modes of Production*, p. 11.

5. Ibid., pp. 9–10.

6. Shanin, *Peasants and Peasant Societies*, p. 13.

7. Ibid., pp. 14–15.

8. See J. Clammer, 'Anthropological Perspectives on Co-operation and Group Farming: Fiji and Southeast Asia', in John Wong (ed.), *Group Farming in Asia* (Singapore: Singapore University Press, 1979).

9. G. M. Foster, 'Peasant Society and the Image of Limited Good', *American Anthropologist*, 2, 1965, pp. 293–315. For a broader discussion of these issues see the papers by Dobrowolski, Bailey and Ortiz, in Shanin, *Peasants and Peasant Societies*, who also provides extensive references to the main literature touching on this topic.

10. Marshall Sahlins, chapters 2 and 3 of *Stone Age Economics* (London: Tavistock Publications, 1972). On Chayanov, see the English translation of his work *The Theory of Peasant Economy*, translated and edited by D. Thorner, R. E. F. Smith and B. Kerblay (Irwin, 1966).

11. See H. Wolpe, 'Capitalism and Cheap Labour-Power in South Africa: From Segregation to Apartheid', *Economy and Society*, vol. 1, no. 4, 1972.

12. Andrew Pearse, 'Metropolis and Peasant: The Expansion of the Urban-Industrial Complex and the Changing Rural Structure', in Shanin, *Peasants and Peasant Societies*, p. 69.

13. In particular, of course, one thinks of the work of Paulo Freire, *Cultural Action for Freedom* and *Pedagogy of the Oppressed*. Both Penguin Books, Hardmondsworth, 1972.

14. Pearse, 'Metropolis and Peasant', p. 79.

15. C.f. William Mangin (ed.), *Peasants in Cities* (Boston: Houghton Mifflin, 1970).

16. E.g. David Bonavia, 'China turns to the consumer', *Far Eastern Economic Review*, vol. 107, no. 10, March 7, 1980, p. 92.

17. On the study of such peasant upheavals see Henry A. Lansberger (ed.), *Rural Protest: Peasant Movements and Social Change* (London: Macmillan, 1974).

18. See, for example, C. Y. Thomas, *Dependence and Transformation* (New York: Monthly Review Press, 1974).

19. For an excellent analysis of many of the problems of this general school of thought see Caroline Hutton and Robin Cohen, 'African Peasants and Resistance to Change: A Reconsideration of Sociological Approaches', in Oxaal, Barnett and Booth, *Beyond the Sociology of Development*, pp. 105–30.

20. For an exposition and commentary on this approach, see the paper by Norman Long, 'Structural Dependency, Modes of Production and Economic Brokerage in Rural Peru', in Oxaal *et al.*, *Beyond the Sociology of Development*, pp. 253–82.

21. See Norman Long and Paul Richardson, 'Informal Sector, Petty Commodity Production, and the Social Relations of Small-scale Enterprise', in J. Clammer (ed.), *The New Economic Anthropology* (London: Macmillan, 1978), pp. 176–209.

22. Joel S. Khan, 'Marxist Anthropology and Peasant Economics: A Study of the Social Structures of Underdevelopment', in J. Clammer, ibid., pp. 110–37. For dissenting views on the nature of petty-commodity production and the informal sector, see P. J. Rimmer, D. W. Drakasis-Smith and T. G. McGee (eds) *Food, Shelter and Transportation in Southeast Asia and the Pacific: Challenging the 'Unconventional Wisdom' of Development Studies in the Third World* (Canberra: Australian National University, 1978).

23. For a clear statement of some of these problems, and in particular the critique of certain conventional views of the peasant, see Sutti Ortiz, 'Reflections on the Concept of "Peasant Culture" and "Peasant Cognitive Systems", in Shanin, *Peasants and Peasant Societies*, pp. 322–35.

24. Shanin, ibid., p. 239.

10   The Anthropological Analysis of Peripheral Capitalism

This chapter has two purposes. The first and most obvious is the attempt to suggest a model of the anthropological characteristics of peripheral capitalist societies. The second – the 'hidden agenda' – is to provide a critique and reformulation of what is usually termed the 'anthropology of complex societies'. It is my belief that the anthropological study of complex societies has, for the most part, failed miserably for a variety of reasons including its continuing entrapment within the structural-functionalist paradigm, its fixation with the methods derived from that particular period of the discipline's development, a self-limiting focus on small-scale social formations and an unwillingness to take seriously several of its allegedly central claims to disciplinary uniqueness – including the concept of totality, the analysis of culture, the comparative method and skill at structural analysis. One theme of this chapter will be that in the analysis of complex societies a return to these betrayed principles will yield much fruit.

The specific theme, however, is a little more limited and concrete: to set about exploring the anthropological characteristics of peripheral capitalist formations. By these I mean those societies which, while geographically and usually culturally removed from the controlling centres of metropolitan capitalism, have themselves taken on the characteristics of centres of secondary concentration and diffusion of the capitalist mode of production. I do *not* mean all those societies peripheral *to* metropolitan capitalism, but only these which have themselves adopted capitalism as their economic and politico-social style. Thus amongst the metropolitan centres of capitalism I would include the USA, Western Europe and especially West Germany, Holland, France, Switzerland and the UK, Australia and Japan. By peripheral capitalist I would mean such states as diverse as Brazil, India, Thailand and Egypt. Additionally, I have in mind the so-called 'gang of four' of East Asia – South Korea, Hongkong, Taiwan and Singapore. Indeed, one of the contemporary euphemisms for peripheral capitalist states is that of 'Newly Industralised (or Industralising) Countries', or NICs, of which these four are classical examples. And it is also my contention that the very 'success' of these four countries makes them highly attractive as models for other 'developing' countries, and as such they require careful scrutiny. My strategy will not be to explore the details of specific histories or current economic structures: I will keep such details in the background while I attempt to set out the general anthropological features of this category of society.

The significance of peripheral capitalist societies in the total structure of world capitalism is very great: they provide the local centres for the reception of metropolis-generated innovations in the system, for the diffusion of the system itself to surrounding pre-capitalist or partially capitalist areas, and they play an important role in the so-called international division of labour in that they provide locations in which capitalism can reproduce itself, repress production costs, encourage the emergence of consumerism and thus stimulate new markets, obtain raw materials, protect itself through decentralisation from localised or regional political instabilities in other areas and generally advance its own interests while representing these as being purely indigenous to the peripheral areas. At the same time, during recession, capital can be withdrawn, investments terminated, local operations restructured, foreign management personnel relocated, all with great ease. This is particularly true of the multinational corporations (MNCs), despite these same MNCs having usually received substantial tax holidays, numerous legal benefits and the provision of physical infrastructures (roads, etc.) at the expense of the host society. But lying behind these abstract characteristics is a sociological reality – that of the impact of peripheral capitalism on the societies, cultures and peoples which, through choice or otherwise, support it.

But we need to begin at a political level – with the question of the 'nation-state'. It is presumably well known by now that the rhetoric of 'nation building' is frequently used for purposes of mystification, which conceals actual economic domination and the construction of political structures serving élite interests. Thus in virtually every peripheral-capitalist social formation there is great emphasis on the integrity of the State – in political, territorial and symbolic terms. The irony is not only that, given the reach of the MNCs, few such countries are really independent, but that virtually every NIC is actually somehow divided: Korea territorially, Taiwan in its dispute with the People's Republic, and others by issues of race, separatism, religion, and so on. The question of the (relatively recent) historical origin of the concept of the nation-state cannot detain us here: what is important is to note its majoor sociological component. This is the emergence of a class or alliance of classes which can create and control a centralised state apparatus which has political and economic domination. The extraction of a surplus (itself the basis of capitalism) and the formation of the state go hand in hand, and in turn create the preconditions for the accumulation of capital and eventual proletarianisation.

These days one tends to talk about these processes in a very abstract way – they happened in Europe a long time ago. But it must be remembered that they are still happening today in the Third World and their effects – displacement of labour, destruction of craft-based industries, widespread internal and external migration, etc. – are still being felt in an acute form: this is still a contemporary process and will indeed continue as such until, if ever, capital expands to its outer limits. What we must seek to do then is to identify and document these effects.

TIME, SPACE AND CAPITALISM

Let us start with a lengthy quotation from Samir Amin which captures perfectly a major, but not often noted aspect of capitalism – its effects on concepts of time:

> A society that wishes to control its future must first and foremost take a long view – have a lengthy 'time-prospect'. This was the case with the precapitalist societies, in which the dominant instance was not the economic but the politico-ideological one. However, these societies had little power over nature, owing to the low level of development of the productive

forces (hence their religious alienation). These societies built pyramids or cathedrals, in other words, monuments that were destined to last forever and the purpose of which was to serve not men but the gods. In capitalist society this claim is made no longer: but while capitalism has freed men from the gods, it has not freed them from themselves. All it can offer them is an alienating ideology, that of the 'consumer society', a short-term prospect of 'growth' of consumption without any reference to real human needs. This shortening of the time-prospect results from the dominant function of the rate of surplus value. It is this rate that determines the pace of accumulation, and so, ultimate, the 'rate of discount' on the basis of which choices are made. It seems to give rationality to what is irrational. But we know that a rate of 7 to 15 per cent means that the alternatives between which a choice has to be made become practically identical within a period of ten to fifteen years at the most. In fact, 'economic calculation' is nothing more than an ideological justification of the way capitalist enterprises spontaneously behave. Even when it is transposed to the national or 'social' scale and purged of its most harmful consequences by taking into consideration 'reference prices', nothing has been done to alter its short-sighted outlook. The crisis of our civilization is wholly concentrated in this absurd contraction of human time. One of its aspects is the contradiction in which our civilization is trapped, between the 'objectives' of education and those of the system of production. In a world that is progressing fast, education cannot content itself with teaching techniques that correspond to particular occupational capacities, which it is hardly possible to know will still be wanted in twenty years' time. Education ought therefore to form men with a capacity, later on and throughout their lives, for adapting themselves and progressing, and also, contrariwise, for adapting economic evolution to the pace they prefer. But this is not the purpose of 'educational planning': a victim of economistic alienation, it tries to treat the formation of human beings as a cost (one of the capitalist enterprise's external savings) and therefore tries to adapt its products to the needs of the economy – needs that the system itself does not know for more than ten or twenty years ahead.[1]

The concept of time (which itself becomes a commodity under capitalism), education, the subordination of value to utility, the

emergence of consumerism all emerge, along with the commoditi-
sation of land, people, natural resources and even open spaces
(the air, the sea). The term the 'consumer society' thus actually
means far more than it first suggests, since it involves not only
consumption as such, but a whole range of changes in culture,
social relationships, the economy and consequently in civilisation
itself. Although it has not yet been fully analysed in these terms,
changes in the perception of space and time, which have hitherto
been considered the responsibility of literacy by commentators
such as the late Marshall McLuhan, may perhaps be seen in this
wider context. In other words, the break down of 'oralcy' and the
emergence of so-called 'linear thinking' and the subsequent
emergence of the technology of mass media – and in particular
television – are actually the result of much profounder social
processes than the spread of literacy (important though it is)
alone. And the basis of these changes – often represented as
objectively progressive ('civilising influences', 'inevitable consequences of progress', etc.) is essentially the spread of capitalism
and the cultural changes that it creates or promotes. Clearly the
detailed documentation of these processes would require a whole
book – but at least here they can be identified.

It is in conjunction with this topic – and in particular with the
short-term quality of planning in the peripheral capitalist systems
which still have acute problems of stability – that the question of
the philosophy of 'pragmatism' arises. Pragmatism is usually
justified as being positively a good thing – as an indication of
flexibility, of the absence of doctrinaire solutions, and so on. But it
has another side to it: that it is a mechanism for removing
ideological debate from the public arena and replacing it with
technical solutions to social problems. Of course, to be without an
ideology is also to be without a theory – without any coherent
picture of how the social entity is evolving. But this is not
especially surprising as it has two sources. The first of these is the
built-in characteristic of a capitalist civilisation as defined by
Amin: it *cannot* plan. The second has been defined as 'action
without theoretical guidance and rooted in pragmatic experience,
spontaneity in the form of hunches, expediency of any means to
the class end, such is the philosophy underlying the making of
state policy'.[2] Pragmatism thus gives away the fact that the
techniques of social engineering and managerialism, so beloved in
peripheral formations, do not actually work: they constantly need

adjustments, reversals, modifications, to make them viable, even in the short term. The attempt to abolish ideology (and with it, politics, especially by appeal to allegedly universal and class free factors such as the 'national interest'), is thus closely tied in with the incidence of political and economic pragmatism and its attractiveness to the managers of peripheral capitalist systems.

EXPANSION AND PLANNING

A key contradiction in any capitalist system is that between the need to produce and the capacity to consume. This contradiction is particularly acute in peripheral systems where purchasing power is low or where the goods produced cannot be culturally assimilated. This obliges the system to promote consumerism by a number of means which include encouragement of the growth of a local bourgeoisie and the stifling of cultural forms which do not easily accept either the goods or the values produced by capitalism. This creates a difficulty: for the internal market to expand wages must increase to raise purchasing power; but rising wages means that the necessity of the system to keep down the cost of labour power declines. Two strategies are possible to deal with this – either export-oriented capitalism, in which the goods produced locally at low cost are not (for the most part) consumed locally, but are exported to higher wage locations, or to promote a further international or regional division of labour by allowing wages to rise, but by concentrating production in high technology, high value added and capital intensive fields, and allowing labour intensive industries to collapse or to migrate to lower cost locations (this later being Singapore's strategy, for instance.) In either case, the law of maintaining the highest possible rate of surplus value is, of course, maintained.

But this is not the whole of the picture – the keeping down of wages, where it occurs, does not exhaust the sociological picture. Indeed, in some cases the wages may have to rise to some extent to satisfy rising expectations which will be reflected in political sentiments, but they will inevitably remain lower than in the metropolitan economies. (A particularly invidious and widespread example of this principle is that of paying Third World crewmen of First World merchant ships wages often as low as one-third of that of the corresponding First World wage – a practice incidently widely condoned by trade unions of seamen in the 'developed' countries.) We have already mentioned the expansion of consumerism necessitated by the expansion of the internal market either for a proportion of the goods produced by international enterprises or by local capitalists. The growth of a bureaucracy to administer this and of a compradore bourgeoisie naturally accompany this process. Indeed, major state intervention in the capitalist economy – whether through state-run enterprises, through regulation of stock exchanges, the banking sector, in the provision of physical infrastructure, tax laws or labour laws – tends always to increase. Luxury consumption, including heavy investment in expensive property and in consumer durables, results. The élite become ever more integrated into the world system, while in many cases the masses experience not development, but increasing relative or even absolute impoverishment. A number of very direct sociological consequences flow from this: proletarianisation of craft workers, breakdown and disappearance of a small-scale family businesses, urbanisation (and a corresponding urban bias in development planning), the expansion of estate agriculture over autonomous peasant farming, marginalisation of rural workers and in many cases un- or underemployment especially amongst vulnerable groups such as women or ethnic minorities. In short, the consequences of the industrial revolution in the West are often experienced all over again in the Third World.

The situation is not, however, precisely the same as that which prevailed in the West – due in part to what has become known as 'the late development effect'. There is already available to Third-World élites a considerable body of experience in managing a capitalist economy. This finds its expression in the technocratic mentality and in the rapid emergence of a new middle class of executives and managers who are entirely loyal to the system which has created them. 'Social engineering' – a process as sinister in reality as its name suggests – becomes pervasive in peripheral formations. The impact of capitalism and its short-term time-cycle unleash a range of social changes which have to be 'managed'. Planning thus becomes basically the enterprise of making sure that the society planned is congruent with the needs of the capitalist system. The expansion of bureaucracy to administer this process is a corollary of this.

THE DIRECT SOCIOLOGICAL EFFECTS

These we can list as follows. (a) The creation through ethnic policies of internal pools of cheap, available labour which can be maintained at little or no cost to the state institutions (as in South Africa).[3] The two main variants on this are internal migration (typically from countryside to industrial cities) or international migration (historically by, for example, Indian labour to the Malayan plantations, or today by Filippino labour to the Middle East and the international market in Asian domestics and electronics workers). (b) Mechanisms for the creation of false needs amongst the masses, the most obvious example of which is advertising. (c) Urbanisation. (d) Tactics for the prevention of politicisation of the workers (through education, government sponsored 'development' programmes, direct repression, the cultivation of myths, the playing off of ethnic groups against one anohter, etc.). (e) Growing inequality and in many cases declining real incomes. (f) Destruction of traditional industries and proletarianisation or marginalisation of those formerly involved in them. A corollary of this is also the replacement of craft produced wares with often inferior mass produced alternatives, and the bending of cultural values to the desiring of objects not hitherto at all congruent with the prevailing culture. (g) Changing occupational (and thus social) structures to accommodate the technological domination of the central economies. In particular, one should consider here the multifaceted effects of the multinational corporations.[4]

(h) Ecological degredation caused by natural resource exploitation (mining, logging, fishing). (i) Emergence of local élites and eventually of an often small but economically significant national bourgeoisie. (j) Creation of economic enclaves such as 'free-trade zones' which, while providing tax and other benefits for the MNCs, frequently also create concentrations of poorly paid, badly housed workers of rural origin, who often suffer considerable adjustment problems to urban–industrial life. (k) Anti-union and generally anti-labour policies designed to create a docile and malleable workforce. (l) Emergence of local economic and political élites either as compradores or parasitic on the capitalist mode of development. (m) A form of economic nationalism entirely antithetical to the emergence of international links amongst the working classes of the peripheral formations. These are often prevented from appearing by legal means. While at the same time the national bourgeoisie, of course, has such links and participates directly in the world economy. (n) There is a tendency for the skills structure of peripheral workforces to be changed. In general, peripheral economies are concerned with three types of activity: primary extraction and/or plantation agriculture; production for export of articles, the technology for which is not indigenous; and service activities. This latter sector, and especially provision for MNCs, tends to grow and as it does so creates great economic vulnerability to shutdowns, recessions, etc., and leads to the progressive depletion of the original base of primary productive activities (i.e. native industries).

(o) Payment of lower wages at the periphery for the same skills and for the same or higher productivity than at the centre. (p) Powerlessness – both on the part of the individual worker and of the indigenous national economy which has no independent means of dealing with international monopolies. The theory of the 'integration' of the world economy and the 'international division of labour' is true only from the centre's perspective: from the periphery it looks much more like dependency. (q) Seemingly contradictory policies towards the so-called 'informal sector', a subject which has attracted considerable attention from sociologists, geographers and anthropologists interested especially in Third World cities. One policy is to suppress the informal sector – with the intention of forcing it to yield up its labour for absorbtion into the formal sector, and at the same time to improve the policing of the labour force by preventing the creation of an 'underground economy'. The alternative is to encourage the informal economy with the intention that it play a vital part in the reproduction of labour using its own resources (and not those of the State or the companies) and thus provide a 'reserve army' or reservoir of potential labour, which, when not needed, supports itself by its own informal activities. Both policies, of course, have a very similar structural intention. Additionally involved here may also be the problem of disguised unemployment common in peripheral formations, and likewise the increase in disguised poverty which is either concentrated in the informal sector (and is thus 'invisible' officially) or which occurs because the suppression of income-generating activities within the informal sector is a serious deprivation for low-income families or individuals. (r) Increasing bureaucracy and bureaucratisation of everyday life. (s) Urban bias in development strategies, and (t) the tendency for the peripheral centres to take on many of the characteristics of the metropolitan centres in relation to their own hinterland.

ANTHROPOLOGICAL INTERPRETATIONS

This list is not exhaustive: it can no doubt be added to with many specific items. But other than simply developing a list, it is also important to attempt to integrate these items into a more totalising picture. A sketch for such a picture will now be attempted. Briefly, the components of this picture are as follows: anthropology has already achieved great success in its analysis of myth. The generation of myths – of economic growth, of security, of stability, of fears of external threats – is a major part of the attempt to legitimate power structures. Two things are required here of the anthropologist: to turn attention from the study of the myths of 'primitive' peoples, and begin systematically to explore the myths of complex ones and to extend the analysis of myth into the realm of the study of ideology. Even as they exist at the moment with their many deficiencies, anthropological methods are well suited for the exploration of ideologies and the realities that underlie them.[5] This in turn leads to the question of methods. There is, of course, no fundamental reason why anthropology should confine itself to the 'primitive', the small scale, the exotic, especially when pressing issues of larger concern are at hand, and especially when these same issues can be very much illuminated by traditional methods. It should be remembered that the original inspiration of anthropology was to be a holistic study of man – sociological, biological, cultural and psychological. Unfortunately, historically, since the rise of functionalism the purely sociological has come to predominate, to the general improverishment of the discipline as a whole.

The question of methods leads itself to that of the selection of problems and ethical commitment. Two issues are really at stake here: the morality of selecting problems of purely academic interest when there are critical issues of practical importance crying out for analysis; and the question of whether as yet the studies carried out by anthropologists have done anything to help in real and concrete terms the people being studied. The 'professional ethics' debate seems to have gone very quiet again in the last few years: in the context of the significance of peripheral capitalist systems it clearly needs reopening.[6] In other words, the question of the problematic of anthropology and its future development must again be seriously reconsidered in the light of the nature of late capitalist social systems. It points to the need for a refurbishing of the holistic claims of anthropology and for a revival of the now almost forgotten discipline of philosophical anthropology: the scrutiny of concepts of human nature and human needs and their relationship to cultural, social, economic and political systems. An inescapable conclusion from this must be that, whatever its critics may have to say about this idea, anthropology to be both professionally sound and ethically respectable must be *critical*.[7] At the present stage of world development this is not an option: it is a necessity.

The critical consideration of peripheral formations also reopens discussion of much-used, but not necessarily well-understood, concepts such as that of 'reproduction', now used in so many senses that it is difficult any longer to define. Reproduction, for instance, has been used in the senses of sexual reproduction, the reproduction of total systems, the reproduction of adequately socialised labour, in relation to ideologies, to the generation of sex-roles, as a means of maintaining the 'meritocracy', of allocation of individuals to class positions, and so on. A priority here has a twofold character: the clarification of each of these senses so that they can be used accurately and rigorously, and the specification of their inter-relationships since related they most certainly are.[8] So called 'socialisation' is not a neutral term, as workers like Basil Bernstein have so convincingly shown. It is rather a device for generating personalities that fit into predetermined moulds, about which the individual 'victim' has no control until it is too late – when she/he is already socialised. This is perhaps especially true in the case of women under peripheral capitalist systems: they are socialised into certain patterns of behaviour and expectations which fit very ill with the realities of their social and cultural positions. Such socialisation may be backed up with legal restraints – on owning property, or even being a 'legal person' at all. This is essentially why women in the labour market are so very vulnerable in the peripheral context: they are peripheral to the periphery! Frequently worse educated than their male counterparts, they are usually worse paid for the same work (and often for higher productivity), frequently forced to take only part-time jobs (as in Japan, for instance), their economic livelihood is at great risk in times of recession and generally form a marginalised group amongst an often already marginalised proletariat. The anthropological analysis of 'reproduction' must take into account all these factors if it is to be adequate or even morally viable. This is only one example: one could extend the analysis to all or most of the central concepts of conventional anthropology.

It is at this point that one also begins to discern a significant convergence between anthropology and, strangely enough, those sociologies which have been hitherto usually been regarded as 'denuded'[9] – the 'sociologies of everyday life'. These we can divide into two categories: critical sociologies and ethnomethodology. The former has to do not only with the description of life as lived and experienced on an everyday basis by the members of the particular society under investigation, but also, as its name suggests, with its *critique*: the depiction of its routines, its ordinariness and its occasional extraordinariness, with people's mechanisms for coping, surviving, prospering, and so on. As such, it transcends the details of everyday life and also attempts to categorise and analyse them: for example, the breakdown of communities and the rise of individualism, the division of labour, the decay of ritual and symbolism, the proliferation of signs, and the general lack of meaning, the degree to which all these can be related to factors such as the growth of bourgeois ideologies and of capitalism, bureaucracy, technology and consumerism, and the emergence of repression.[10] The weakness of this approach is that so far it has confined itself to analysing the (by Third World standards) highly affluent lifestyles of the West, and even of the so-called 'post-industrial society'. This is rather a sick joke from the point of view of the periphery, which is really where the method needs rigorously applying. But on the positive side it indicates that the link between anthropology and critical sociology, which has not yet been forged, offers a potentially very powerful tool for the analysis of 'complex societies'. The other dimension to this is that of ethnomethodology: at first sight as far from the issues being discussed here as one can get. But actually this is not entirely so; since ethnomethodology can also be seen as a method for the analysis of everyday life and of life worlds, of uncovering the processes of ideological reproduction, and as such providing the 'ethnographic data'[11] for the more comprehensive investigation to which it must be assimilated.

What all this points to is that in dealing with peripheral capitalist formations we are dealing with a *system*: both in the sense that these formations have regularly found identifiable features of the kind discussed in this paper, and in the sense that peripheral capitalism is itself part of a wider world system from which it cannot be detached. Methodologically this points to the need for a new (non-Lévi-Straussian) definition of structuralism as a synthesis of the features of the system (especially the world system) and of ethnographic data appropriate to the analysis of concrete problems. This suggests a critique of the conventional 'anthropology of complex societies', which has tended to be little more than the study by conventional means of those facets of urban or industrialised societies which look 'traditional' to the anthropologists – kinship, street corners, slums, 'tribesmen-in-cities', and so on. That this approach is clearly inadequate to the genuine study of the modern world has been one of the thrusts of this paper.[12] The alternative that I am suggesting involves a structural approach, linkages above to the world systems analysis and linkages below to the analysis of everyday life. Central to this approach – and indeed the element which really holds the whole thing together – is the analysis of ideology and the reproduction of ideological systems. It is at this point that much of the insight of traditional anthropology can be retained, for instance the analysis of myth, since the generation of myths – of security, law and order, modernisations and development, and so on – is central to the maintaining of the social systems of peripheral capitalism. But hitherto the anthropological study of myth has focused on their internal structure and their role in the resolution of contradictions (in the minds of the mythologues). What it has not yet done is to examine myth as mystification, as mechanisms of domination, of the 'resolution' of contradictions in the mind but not in society.

The answer to this lies in the examination of consciousness itself and its interplay with its social context – with, in effect, the anthropology of knowledge. It is precisely this that allows the link between structure and everyday life to be made. Systems of domination – sexism, racism, class, inequalities, systems of symbolism, the State itself, all of which are often represented as 'natural' or just part of the 'real world', as 'inevitable' – can thus be brought to the foreground of the anthropological consciousness, analysed and criticised. Hence ideological analysis has very practical consequences since it enables individuals and groups to overcome the situation described as follows: 'Thus the ideology blurs the real differences between the real positions of different dominated groups. The ideology can deny the dominated to authentically represent their own domination.'[13] The treatment of contradictions and the re-analysis of some central themes of critical sociology – such as that of alienation – thus become possible.

All this may seemingly have brought us a long way from our theme of the anthropological concomitants of peripheral capitalist systems. But I would argue that in reality it has not. The whole issue raises not merely empirical questions – what are such systems like? – but also and inevitably methodological questions, moral questions, conceptual questions and the whole issue of what anthropology is and what it thinks it is doing in the late twentieth century. The empirical and the theoretical issues fit together: this is *praxis*. And while no final solution is possible or is offered here, perhaps the outlines of some of the ways forward can be discerned, by way of this sketch, for the analysis of a major and growing type of social formation.

NOTES AND REFERENCES

1. Samir Amin, *Unequal Development: An Essay on the Social Formations of Peripheral Capitalism* (New York and London: Monthly Review Press, 1976), pp. 70–1.
2. H. K. Wells, *Pragmatism* (New York, 1954), p. 207.
3. Harold Wolpe, 'Capitalism and Cheap Labour Power in South Africa: From Segregation to Apartheid', *Economy and Society*, vol. 1, no. 4, 1972.
4. This issue has been tackled by a group of anthropologists. See Ahamed Idris-Soven, Elizabeth Idris-Soven and Mary K. Vaughan (eds), *The World as a Company Town: Multinational Corporations and Social Change* (The Hague and Paris: Mouton, 1978).
5. See for example Pierre Bourdieu, 'Symbolic Power', *Critique of Anthropology*, 4, nos 13–14, 1979.
6. For some reflections on this see Gerrit Huizer, 'Anthropology and Multinational Power: Some Ethical Considerations on Social Research in the Underdeveloped Countries', in Idris-Soven *et al.*, *The World as a Company Town*.
7. For an argument against the critics of this point of view see Bob Scholte, 'Critical Anthropology since its Reinvention', in Joel S. Kahn and Josep R. Llobera (eds), *The Anthropology of Pre-Capitalist Societies* (London: Macmillan, 1981).

8. Two useful sources might be cited here. The first is Olivia Harris and Kate Young, 'Engendered Structures: Some Problems in the Analysis of Reproduction', in Kahn and Llobera, ibid. The second is P. Bourdieu and J-C, Passeron, *Reproduction in Education, Society and Culture* (London and Beverley Hills: Sage, 1977) (Sage Studies in Society and Educational Change, Vol. 5).
9. E.g. by Peter Worsley: 'The State of Theory and the Status Theory', *Sociology*, 8, 1, 1974.
10. Perhaps the most coherent account is to be found in Henri Lefebvre, *La vie quotidienne dans la monde moderne* (Paris: Gallimard, 1968). English translation, *Everyday Life in the Modern World* (London: Allen Lane, The Penguin Press, 1971). Also relevant here are the works of H. Marcuse.
11. On this theme see Beng-Huat Chua, 'Delineating a Marxist Interest in Ethnomethodology', *The American Sociologist*, 12, 1977.
12. For example the book by Peter L. Berger, Brigette Berger and Hansfried Kellner, *The Homeless Mind: Modernization and Consciousness* (Harmondsworth: Penguin Books, 1977), teems with ideas that the anthropologist might take up.
13. Steve Barnett and Martin G. Silverman, *Ideology and Everyday Life* (Ann Arbor: University of Michigan Press, 1979). (A book which despite its seemingly 'sociological' title is written by two anthropologists).

11 Development Anthropology and the Study of Poverty: A Note

One of the key areas of concern to development anthropologists has been the study of poverty: indeed to some people this subject is almost synonymous with development anthropology. The way the problem is seen, however, has undergone considerable changes. As a major focus of interest poverty largely dates from the works of Oscar Lewis and the subsequent 'culture of poverty' debate. Essentially this revolved around the legitimacy of studying poverty as, or as if it were, a culture – an integrated, self-sustaining and self-regulating lifestyle – without attention to its causes and its eradication. As a consequence of this debate interest switched to a great extent to, on the one hand, a more refined conceptualisation of the problem itself (for example the emergence of the idea of the 'informal sector'), and on the other, the development of more rigorous explanatory models – including structural ones, Marxist theories of exploitation and alienation, and a general decline in individualist, psychological or cultural explanations of poverty. The current trend in development anthropology is undoubtedly towards an action-oriented approach: that is, seeing poverty not as something to be merely *studied*, but as a social evil to be eradicated. The role of the anthropologist becomes that, not of the dispassionate observer (as in traditional fieldwork methods), but of the analyst of the sociological, cultural, ecological and other factors causing the situation of poverty, and the recommender of appropriate strategies to eradicate poverty while causing, wherever possible, the least socio-cultural damage. He may even become a partisan – an individual committed to the destruction of poverty, if necessary by political means.

What then are the typical components of the action approach to poverty? The first point is surely that it is concerned not only with contributing to the solution of the poverty problem in the particular location involved, but that it does so at three levels, seemingly separate, but which actually closely articulate. These are: (i) at the level of the perceptions, strategies, feelings and life-ways of those who are poor; (ii) at the level of structural features of the society and economy within which the poverty is encapsulated; and (iii) at the level of the policy-makers, planners, social workers and other agencies who mediate, or attempt to, between the first and second levels. Of necessity the micro and macro levels have to be linked, or, to put it in more conventional anthropological terms, the approach must be holistic. This holistic approach automatically enables us to dispense with the idea that poverty is caused by a single factor – for example (and pupularly), cultural constraints on saving and capital formation such as feasting. Often in fact one sees it as being the other way round – that poverty creates a social environment in which consumption rather than accumulation is necessary, and that often the whole syndrome is linked to such factors as disruption of a traditional economy by the appearance of wage-labour, landlessness, caste affiliation or unemployment whether of the more obvious or the disguised varieties.

In turn, a number of important practical and methodological consequences flow from this. One of these would be the rejection of urban bias in favour of a more balanced view of the distribution of poverty. Another would be the recognition that if a holistic approach to understanding poverty is necessary, so is a holistic approach to doing something about it. This implies the involvement of those affected by the poverty and by alleviation programmes: in other words, that the poor are not just 'clients' but active participants in their own futures and in determining the sorts of policies towards them that they find just, efficient and culturally acceptable. The anthropologist is, or should be, uniquely placed to help in this situation, which is really a process of communication, given his usual taste for and training in grass roots concerns combined with a theoretical training in understanding social processes as a whole.

For example, the poor do not usually just sit still and do nothing about their situation, despite some conventional views of fatalism and apathy. On the contrary, they have endlessly ingenious strategies for coping. These strategies are not only or necessarily the result of desperation, but are often the fruit of wisdom and long experience. They are adaptive for example, flexible, are based on a close understanding of local ecological conditions, and often represent more or less the maximum that can be achieved given available technology and other resources. The way out of poverty may very well not lie in sweeping away such accumulated folk knowledge, but rather in building on it, in discovering and removing the bottlenecks to greater productivity and in adjusting the relationships between the community concerned and the wider social scene – for example, by legal provision of access to land, water, housing or other resources, by the creation of marketing networks for surplus produce, or by attempting to control the unrestrained inrush of 'modernization' with its attendant dislocations, and, paradoxically, often poverty creating innovations (for example, the 'Green Revolution' in some parts of the world).

In short, the action approach to a development anthropology understanding of, and potential solution to, poverty stresses several key factors: the intelligence and cultural integrity of the underprivileged; an understanding of their survival strategies and the ways to build on those they have already tried and tested; an attempt to build bridges of communication between the poor with *their* perception of their situation, and the policy-makers and implementors with theirs with the intention of reconciling these views; analysis of the structural factors creating and sustainiing the poverty with a view to removing such obstacles, opening channels to resources hitherto denied the poor, and promoting institutionalised ways of linking development at the macrolevel with development at the microlevel.

While such an approach calls upon all the traditional skills of the anthropologist – participant observation, rapport with informants, sensitivity and rigorous microlevel data collection – it also requires the linking of these skills to others such as socio-economic systems analysis, understanding of broader historical and economic processes bearing on the particular unit of analysis, ability to utilise network approaches for studying patron–client relationships and a grasp of the political realities underlying the creation and perpetuation of poverty. As such it must be recognised that this kind of development anthropology is not really something radically new – a total reshaping of the discipline. Rather it is a fulfilment of the discipline's claim to holism – to treat the economic, political, cultural, religious and social dimensions of a society as a single and interlocking system. Development problems possess exactly this holistic character. What is a 'basic need', for example, may depend on who is defining it and what exactly is its content and its mode of delivery. Housing, yes, but what kind? Health care, yes, but of what sort? Education, yes, but with what content? The development anthropologist in studying poverty has immensely powerful methodological tools in his grasp if he knows how to use them. The study of poverty and its requirement that it *defines* poverty, identifies the groups who are poor (women? landless labourers? children?), understands their perception of their situation, links this to structural factors and mediates between people and policy-makers is perhaps in the most advantageous position of any discipline to make a concerted, serious, realistic, practically effective and intellectually and theoretically sound contribution to understanding the phenomenon of poverty and alleviating it.

Index

171

172 *Index*